A Singer
of Memory

A Sinner of Memory

ESSAYS BY
Melita Schaum

Michigan State University Press • *East Lansing*

Copyright © 2004 by Melita Schaum

g green press INITIATIVE Michigan State University Press is a member of the Green Press Initiative and is committed to developing and encouraging ecologically responsible publishing practices. For more information about the Green Press Initiative and the use of recycled paper in book publishing, please visit *www.greenpressinitiative.org.*

∞ The paper used in this publication meets the minimum requirements of ANSI/NISO Z39.48-1992 (R 1997) (Permanence of Paper).

Michigan State University Press
East Lansing, Michigan 48823-5245
Printed and bound in the United States of America.

09 08 07 06 05 04   1 2 3 4 5 6 7 8 9 10

LIBRARY OF CONGRESS CATALOGING-IN-PUBLICATION DATA
Schaum, Melita, 1957–
A sinner of memory : essays / by Melita Schaum.
p. cm.
ISBN 0-87013-707-7 (cloth : alk. paper)
1. Schaum, Melita, 1957– 2. Poets, American—20th century—Biography.
3. Children of immigrants—United States—Biography. 4. German American
women—Biography. I. Title.
PS3619.C335Z474 2004
811'.6—dc22
2004000269

Cover design by Heather Truelove Aiston
Book design by Sharp Des!gns, Inc., Lansing, Michigan

Cover artwork is *Phoenix Recumbent* by Imogen Cunningham
(© The Imogen Cunningham Trust) and is used with permission. For more information
on the work of Imogen Cunningham please visit *www.imogencunningham.com.*

Visit Michigan State University Press on the World Wide Web at: *www.msupress.msu.edu*

Contents

Author's Note

" . . . like one
Who having into truth, by telling of it,
Made such a sinner of his memory
To credit his own lie. . . ."

        —William Shakespeare, *The Tempest, Act I, Scene 2 (99–103)*

T HE TERM CREATIVE NONFICTION IS A BROAD ONE, AND THE ESSAY form in particular has emerged as a supple genre, spanning narrative and reflection, invention and analysis, in an effort to reach the truce of insight.

Of all literary forms, the personal essay may be one of the more important for us today, in a culture that overwhelms with ready-made opinions and pre-packaged desires. Through telling and reflecting we have a chance to revisit emotional truths, to reclaim the subtleties of experience. It's a tall order—the return to authenticity—but if any form can rise to it, I believe the contemporary essay can.

Having said that, let me add that in Creative Nonfiction, the authentic and the factual may not always be the same. The pieces that follow begin and end in truth, though the route they take between those points may be more vague. I have taken certain liberties with places, names, and details, though I've tried to keep faith with core realities. Still, as with Shakespeare's Antonio, the usurping Duke of Milan—who repeated his own self-serving version of events so often he began to believe it himself—facts have a way of serving the latest master. Vigilant as we may be, making a sinner of memory may be a failing no writer entirely escapes.

I am grateful to the many people and organizations who helped this book along, in particular the Byrdcliffe Arts Colony, the Dorland Mountain Arts Colony, Hawthornden Castle International Writer's Retreat, and the Millay Colony for the Arts, for their precious gifts of time and space; to the University of Michigan–Dearborn and the Institute for Research on Gender at the University of Michigan–Ann Arbor, for funds to complete portions of the book; and to *New Letters Magazine*, *New Millennium Writings*, and *The Literary Review*, for their generous prizes to individual essays in this collection.

Although there are many individuals who deserve thanks, I am especially beholden to Trish Hampl, John Matthias, Kevin Oderman, and Grace Paley, for their wonderful insights and support. Finally, dedications are private things, and they alone know to whom they belong. I send this one to V.—"without whom, etc."—and to J., for all the brave new worlds.

A Singer
of Memory

Falling Bodies

PARIS, I HEAR, IS A CITY OF THE DEAD. IN VENICE THEY HAVE OBIT-
uary photos of the deceased on building walls—the census of
a second, ghostly population that is departed but not gone. Paris's
dead are less civil, more unruly. Piling up in overfilled graveyards in
the eighteenth century, corpses began to be stacked several deep, or
disinterred from rotting boneyards only to be shipped to charnel
houses throughout the city, where they pestered their living neighbors
with the pervasive, suffocating reek of death. Near Les Halles, cavernous mass graves collapsed, jettisoning cadavers into the basements
of horrified homeowners, and one night in 1776, legend has it, a cob-
bler walking across the Cimetière des Innocents tripped in the dark
and plummeted into an open grave, where he was found the next
morning, stone dead, martyr to the cause of civic improvement. Who
was he, this fallen, falling man? Memorials leave him nameless. I'll call
him something historic: Jean-Baptiste Plongeur, diver into death. A
strange Nekuia, unplanned tourist to the Underworld. And where is
he buried now? Surely they didn't leave him where he landed? The
record is silent.

. . .

I DIDN'T SO MUCH ARRIVE IN PARIS AS TUMBLE INTO IT. THE FIRST THING
that happened was that I broke the law. Frowsy and jet-lagged and
speckled with the flak of airline snacks, I dragged my three idioti-
cally massive suitcases of dinnerwear and books along endless cor-
ridors to the railway ticket office, just below the giant glass and

plastic entrails of the Charles de Gaulle airport. The cashier punched out a tiny paper *billet*, pointed me towards the turnstiles that led to the railway platforms. "The train is coming just now," she said. "Next one in one hour."

I hurried towards the bank of turnstiles. With my last energy, I shoved my luggage under the steel bars, inserted the ticket into the automated slot. The tag went in. I jammed my waist against the handles, but the contraption, with immense Gallic indifference, remained frozen. I leaned my hipbones against it, shoved. Nothing. I looked at my bags on the far side, at the train that was just then pulling up. I looked back to the cashier window fifty yards behind me, where a line of at least a dozen tired passengers had formed. I hesitated only long enough to glance to either side like a cartoon burglar, then jumped the turnstile in my heels, purse flapping, imagining the sound of sirens and shouting airport guards and baying dogs starting up behind me.

The train to the Gare du Nord was as empty as the coach car in Joyce's "Araby." By the first few stops through Paris's northwest suburbs, however, it began to fill up—with working girls and Arabic boys, kids with skateboards and huge women in Senegalese prints—until soon it was evident that my luggage was breaking another edict, causing a human traffic jam, crammed as it was into the aisle and opposite seat. A nice Iranian woman squeezed in across from me, deftly pushing one of my suitcases high into the window well.

"You get a man to help you," she said, pointing to my bags. "Many strong men here." She nodded at the gangly boys, none of whom looked especially helpful. She seemed to know I was American. "You are in Paris the first time?"

"*Non, Madame*—" I began to explain in my fitful French, realizing too soon that I'd stepped off a linguistic gangplank and into a conversational abyss I had neither the vocabulary nor the grammar to negotiate. I was spending a month in the City of Light, renting the studio of someone I knew—an evasive, high-strung man, taken to messy divorces and expressionist art. I was cornering myself into yet another creative space in a foreign country in order to write. It had become a habit with me, dragging my manuscripts to cabins in the Alto Adige, stone granges in Brittany, shacks on the Isle of Skye, as if my words needed to be corralled into some refracted foreign space before they'd let themselves be harnessed.

"Friend," I mumbled. "A friend renting." The woman smiled generously and nodded. "*Paris, c'est trés belle,*" I concluded lamely. "*Oui,*" she breathed as we both gazed out at the graffiti and trash-strewn walls of Mitry-Claye.

. . .

STRANGE, WHAT WORKS UP FROM UNDERGROUND. AT MY HOUSE IN Michigan, inexplicable things turn up in the yard: toys unearthed from the loam of the garden, a small action figure, a blue truck with three wheels. Pieces of root and wood disinter from an old cotton-wood that used to stand just where my bulbs are now, and the grass still burps up concrete chunks from a playset jackhammered out of the lawn thirteen years ago.

The earth is bad at keeping secrets. Two years ago my neighbor Ray died of his third stroke. That spring, his wife discovered tiny mass graves of forbidden cigarette butts and little airline bottles of whiskey buried behind the shed.

I found a British sixpence piece in the compost once, a black plastic comb and a girl's barrette; and in my raspberry patch one spring a frozen wiener in a plastic baggie, although that could have been a more recent leaving. Like the enigma of the single shoe lying on the highway median, I could not imagine for what purpose any adult or child would have been carrying or tossing away one bare hot-dog, chilled to the color of eraser rubber, in its own Ziploc bag.

"What's the difference between flotsam and jetsam?" a friend's child asked me once. She, who at five perceptively noticed that flamingos' knees bent backwards. I told her about Hawaiian fishermen finding glass globes from Japan, or the cargo of rubber ducks that broke up around Greenland, sending hundreds and hundreds of yellow bath toys drifting down the Gulf Stream. She liked that.

Before I left for France, she helped me plant peas in the wet March garden. I've taught her how to push the wrinkled orbs into the friable mud. Her fingers are the perfect size for the job, and she's delighted and efficient, poking steady as a rock drill, racing me down the row. As we work, she tells me about finding a dime in a riverbank, and when I point out the pun, she laughs.

In the yard, strange white roots and mushy, overwintered tubers have already begun to send green tongues into the air. Life teems down there. I catch the edge of something and pull—like a message in a bottle, an empty seed packet of something planted here long before I ever moved in.

"What are these?" the child asks at one point, holding her hand up to my face. I look down at two grey, primordial nubs piloting themselves across the unfamiliar terrain of her palm.

"Wood lice."

"What are they for?"

"What do you think they're for?"

"To eat," she says, then sticks out her tongue in disgust, pink as a cat's.

I know that I will never have a child. This truth surfaces like something hard, palpable, incongruous. I'm forty-four. My lover, tangled in the frayed ends of a previous marriage, doesn't want more children now. Peas are the only thing my yard will grow.

I don't know exactly how I feel about this; I think our lives come up at us sometimes in fragments, inexplicably. There we are. There it is.

I turn back to the moist earth. There is so much to bury even before it's born. Somewhere in my heart is a vague, cold ache, but it hasn't worked its way up yet. Its season too will come.

. . .

THE GARE DU NORD WAS THE END OF THE LINE. BOBBING LIKE CORKS on a human tide, my luggage and I surged past a flotilla of train platforms, through the tiny metal exit gates, up the stairwell, and into the blare of rush hour traffic on rue du Faubourg Saint-Denis, a great slap of noise and fumes and the anemic wet daylight I suddenly knew had been a repressed part of all my memories of Paris.

The taxi took me down broad avenues past the Hôpital Lariboisière, under the skeletal Metro overpass at La Chapelle that marks the dividing line between the ninth and eighteenth *arrondissements*. I peered out the windows as the clean, tree lined boulevards, with their gauntlet of watch stores and home boutiques, changed to the gray pavement of Barbès-Rochechouart and the bin-diving anarchy of Tati department store, where Arabic women in veils rummaged through street-side hampers filled with cheap push-up bras and children's clothing. We crept along streets lined with mosques and Muslim butchers, stores that advertised prayer shawls and hair cream. The driver turned up a narrow street past a brick abbey, and a square where the flowing, watery line of one of Paris's last two Hector Guimard metro signs left its cursive, art nouveau signature on space. Above us, the titanic white wedding-cake of a church emerged, perched on a hill along which a tiny funicular traveled up and down like the catch on a zipper.

A maze of one-ways finally brought us to the corner of rue Chappe, a street named, I learned later, for an inventor who committed suicide by throwing himself into a sewer. My building, no. 17, loomed a face of wet bricks at a small ceramic repair shop across the way. A woman in bifocals painting *faïence* looked up as the cab doors slammed. The street was pitched so steeply, my luggage almost rolled away. To my left, a flight of some two hundred steps stretched vertiginously up, past gaslights and tiny wayside gardens, to the teeming plaza of Saint-Pierre that unfurled like an apron around the basilica of Sacré-Coeur. To my right, the cobbled avenue descended sharply past a minuscule restaurant, a lamp store, and an apartment building covered in scaffolding, down to the intersection of the rue des Trois Frères, where clots of tourists thronged on the brief pilgrimage from the Métro station to the sandwich stands and carnival rides at the basilica's base and back again. I looked up at the impassive façade of my home for the next four weeks and, parting with too big a tip, shouldered my luggage and went in.

When I finally fought my way through the studio door's three locks—one of which took a skeleton key the size of a turkey bone to open—I was met by a wave of stale air and dust, the smell of rotting dairy and plumbing. The studio consisted of a bathroom just wide enough for a lidless, rust-encrusted toilet, and a shower stall whose curtain bloomed with extravagantly colored molds. The kitchen, no larger, held a two-burner gas camping stove perched atop a tiny, phlegmatic refrigerator, and a sink full of standing water in which floated the slimy remains of vegetable parings, eggshells, and what looked to be some ancient rinds of cheese. The smell could have stripped paint.

I opened the window and promptly knocked a dead potted plant off the sill to crash on the cement three floors below. The main room looked out onto the blank, unflappable gaze of a dozen other apartment windows, and down on a gray, featureless courtyard as sunless as the bottom of a well. Seven floors up, a tiny square of pewter-colored sky nosed through.

Where were the French doors overlooking a Fabergé-blue sky? The sinuous architectural lines of Broussard? Piano music? I had always imagined a studio in Paris to be an airy, sun-filled space, like something from a Joni Mitchell song. Instead, I had just stepped onto the set of *Trainspotting*—walls the color of tobacco spit, dust balls the size of tumbleweeds.

And that grey, grey sky.

. . .

It wasn't as if we hadn't considered a child. Four years ago we even made an appointment at a fertility clinic, just to take the lay of the land. It had been a rainy morning then, too—I woke to find my lover mopping the kitchen floor where my ceiling had leaked overnight. From behind, he looked so fragile, at forty-nine already weathered through one life, stiffening to shoulder a second. Love started up somewhere in my chest, an ache like unspilled tears.

It had rained all night—liquid, plashing, the air wet and weighted, first light almost imperceptible against the gunmetal-gray sky. The swollen burls of the big maples in my backyard were slick and black with rain, and the alders drooped as if heavy with their own deepened color. It should have been a sign of fertility: in films and books the downpour breaks the arid time of waiting, lovers falling into each other's arms, diving into passion like a pool. But for us, it only made us sleep fitfully and wake to a puddle of water on the kitchen floor. My house, mutely resentful and old, no longer willing to keep us dry.

Over breakfast we drew up and rehearsed our questions for the doctor: blood tests, banks, and cyclotrons, eggs on ice like blue-chip stocks in a fluctuating market. My lover wrote down his concerns and queries on a legal pad, then rearranged them in order of importance as if he were designing a lecture. He worked intently, humorlessly, covering his paper with the crook of his arm like a student taking a test.

I doodled on my page. The edges of my list curled where I'd been rolling them absentmindedly. In my own appalling handwriting—spidery, unstable as a recidivist's—I read:

1. *Can we afford this?*
2. *What are the risks of deformity*
   A. *In the fetus?*
   B. *In the mother?*

I had just turned forty, and time had begun to pull on me like spare luggage, but my real questions had nothing to do with the body's age. I was more interested in the heart, how *its* history presses and reshapes the waiting spaces we have inside. Sometimes I felt like a tree with too many rings, my wooden heart too gnarled by now, my bark too rough to break for some new shoot. I wanted to ask the doctor, a man with a face as calm as a contractor's, what it would take to fix this grudging house, this leaky, uninhabitable shelter.

When we arrived at the clinic, a receptionist took our names and pointed us to a waiting room of mauve chairs and low tables. Periodically, nurses appeared in uniforms printed with teddy bears and called out the name of the next patient: "Maria Trefalis . . . Jane Conover . . . Hiawatha Hindoo." *Hiawatha Hindoo?!* I mouthed at my lover, laughing. Over his shoulder, a television set bolted against the ceiling quacked cartoons. A fat man nearby toyed with a cell phone, absently rubbing his belly as if he too were big with child. This was all too absurd. I reached for a magazine from the swill of parenting journals on the coffee table. Each cover sported a baby's airbrushed face, so that the low, round table looked like a full, cheeping nest.

All we really had were questions, but when we were called, it was difficult to make this clear to the nurses, who briskly took my weight, temperature, blood pressure, and pushed a gown in my direction. *No*, we kept saying over and over, *we're not here for an exam.* An intern came to take a battery of information—about genetic diseases, drug use, alcohol, medical histories. She turned to me. "Have you ever been pregnant before?" The question caught me off guard. "No." My mouth soured. Something in my voice left a tick of silence in the room.

Twenty-two years fell away inside me like a house of cards, and the space they left was full of the light of a shapely August morning glinting off a glass café table, splashing over the petunias that trailed velvet capes from window boxes all down the Kanalstrasse. Across the street brooded the tall Hanseatic house, blind and proper as a brick-clad matron, the makeshift clinic into which a procession of pale young women—some with boyfriends, most alone—had disappeared throughout the span of the morning. Some, like me, had come to this café afterwards, where the proprietor was kind and let us sit as long as we needed to. Just then, unasked, he had brought me a small pastry on a plate. *Please eat. For me.* As if he were the father of us all, us fallen girls in our careless passion and illicit sorrow, there among the sunlit flowers, the day, almost in spite, as beautiful as a box of jewels.

I was certain that I could never reveal this to my lover. This knowledge stunned me, put a curious fissure into the shape of things. It wasn't that he would condemn me—on the contrary, he would probably praise my good sense. The real secret I hid from him was subtler, had to do with risk and error—something a man who came early to airports, who tested the batteries on fire alarms once a month could never understand.

"We just want to get our cross hairs on this," he was saying. The doctor had come in, and the two chatted like old sportsmen. My lover brought up bell curves, percentages; the doctor countered with the relative merits of amniocentesis. My heart felt noisy as a gavel. "I don't mean to make you worry," the doctor smiled. "But if you're serious about this, the sooner you start, the better."

. . .

OTHER GHOSTS HAD FOLLOWED ME TO PARIS. I REALIZED THIS WHEN, that first week, a friend phoned me from the States, desperate to talk about his fear of death. The transatlantic line was crackly, the connection sporadic, as if he were already calling from another world. He had vague symptoms he felt sure were signs of cancer. Pains in his stomach. General fatigue. Two of his friends had died in the past six months—one of lung cancer, one man in his thirties of Hodgkin's lymphoma. Now he was sure that he'd be next. How could I explain to him that fear, not death, is the contagion?

Holding the phone to my ear, I stared out at the bricks streaming in rain that had been falling without remission since I arrived. Across the way, despondent houseplants drooped on balconies, a young cat hunched on a ground-floor windowsill. Behind me the studio's one skinny floor lamp gave off nicotine-colored light onto the rattrap of a sofa that doubled as a bed, and dingy wallpaper that smelled faintly of menthol and Gauloises.

I listened to my friend clamping his fear into words, pushing them down the thin wire of the phone line to try to tame their panicked bucking. Where do our terrors come from? The self against itself—knowing that the mind betrays, that the body is what kills us. I didn't tell him, but for the last six weeks I had been having visions of a woman who, years ago, had been my dearest friend. She died four months ago of a complicated illness called scleroderma—her own skin thickening out of control, growing calloused, entombing her.

We had been estranged for almost ten years, so the news of her death, when it came, was like a report from someplace far away. It was Christmas. I had been unable to grieve. Now the shock seemed to be thawing with the spring, and I had begun seeing her apparition everywhere—a reflection in a shop window, the profile of someone on the street—my mind playing its own tricks of bereavement and resurrection. And she had followed me to Paris. Just that morning in a *boulangerie* I was certain I'd spotted her, but before I could move or call out, the person turned the face of a stranger towards me, and in that instant I remembered—again, again—that my friend was dead.

The irony is that Jackie had always wanted to travel to Paris, yet never had. She'd never visited Europe, or anywhere else for that matter, though she often spoke of longing to go on voyages. Nothing was stopping her—she had the money, and as academics we certainly had the time—but something held her immobile, doomed to while away the long, boring summers in our university's air-conditioned research library, complaining about how fast the days flipped off the calendar until it was time for classes to start again.

One evening she told me she'd had a premonition that she would die young. She had three strong, successful brothers, but her mother had been mad, and her father, ravaged by cancer, had died a grueling death. She felt certain that she herself would be the last sacrifice of a family split into halves: three survivors, three fallen. We were having dinner in her kitchen. I listened, watching her play with the salt shaker as she spoke, laying it on its side and spinning it so that the salt broadcast on the tabletop in an arc, then drawing a wavery line through it with her index finger as if she were trying to trace for me the outline of this unnamable fear. But sitting with her there, I was so sure we would grow old together, convinced I could see us both in forty years—two funny, cynical crones—that I broke the moment, laughed, and waved my hand in the air, poured us each another glass of wine. We fell out not long afterwards over some irrelevant, forgettable quarrel and didn't speak for the next ten years. She died at forty-nine.

Now I listened to the man who had called to offer me his terrors, and my heart quivered with love and helplessness. Who was I to contradict or comfort him? The rain splashed down from a gray cube of sky. Is the moment all there is? I thought of Thelonious Monk playing his silky, rumpled jazz or drinking in the Café de Seine near Saint-Germain. *Il n'y a plus d'après* . . . the melody meanders, sinuous and fatalistic. There is no afterwards.

. . .

THE NEXT DAY, I EMBARKED ON A SPIN OF OBLIGATORY SIGHTSEEING, traipsing dutifully through the Louvre, enduring the crush of Notre Dame. I gazed at the Venus de Milo's abbreviations, at Saint-Denis the martyr on the cathedral's façade, carrying his head like a football. Paris was beginning to seem like a city of missing parts.

At the Conciergerie, I gawked at the guillotine blade, learned that Marie Antoinette, imprisoned here before her execution, had confided that her greatest hardship was not the fear of death, but the low door of her cell, designed so that she would have to bow to her jailers each time she passed its threshold.

"Do you understand this humiliation?" our tour guide barked, squinting over our group: a dozen wide-eyed Americans in sock garters and Hawaiian shirts who'd shelled out the entrance fee to see the dungeons. "No, of course you don't."

She herself—a heavy girl from Brittany trying to hide a lumpy figure under layers of Parisian style—interrogated us like a school-mistress.

"Do you know what caused the period we call *La Terreur?* No, of course you don't. Do you wish me to tell you? *Bien sûr,* of course you do."

We trailed behind her, in and out of jail cells.

"This looks like our hotel room," one woman muttered. "I *told* my husband not to go with anything under three stars."

We crammed into an exhibit area the size of a sauna. A glimpse of Robespierre's slender, lethal signature; a flash of Marie Antoinette's prayer book; an oil painting of the girl who'd drowned Marat in his tub. We bottlenecked into the chapel, crushing a young Japanese couple against the wall with our passing. Emerging in the dank, sacral space we clustered around the guide like convicts.

She pointed out the prison yard where the female inmates had congregated; the courtyard where tumbrels waited to haul off the next unlucky twelve; the table where hair was cut, the better to make the blade fall clean, and sold each week by the basketful to wigmak-ers for a few extra *sous.* I thought of the barristers and judges in their robes, powdered and curled, wearing the hair of the ones they had killed.

It was a cold April, even for Paris. I caught a bus for Les Halles—a wheezing, overheated conveyance that smelled of lozenges and damp wool. Not far from the public gardens' long horizon of trees, I wandered into a beautiful museum: a series of exhibit halls filled with machines, monuments to the exquisite intricacies of human invention. In room after room, glass cases commemorated the evolution of the camera, the printing press, steam engine, computer. Da Vinci was there, as were Eastman and Daguerre. Foucault's pendulum hung, a shining futuristic bauble, in a restored twelfth-century chapel among unicycles, flying machines, and flivvers.

I drifted to a strange apparatus unnoticed by the tourists and school groups that had come to ogle Foucault's famous orb. It was a peculiar contraption: a tall cone comprised of wooden panels, resembling a slender teepee with a platform attached to the top. Its plaque read simply, "Machine to Gauge the Laws of Falling Bodies." Both the appliance and its plate were gorgeously engraved—edged with filigrees of brass, inscribed with the signatures of its creators. I marveled at the superfluity of beauty on something so mundane as a device for testing gravity. I looked at it for a long time, imagining the scientist atop the tower, holding, like God, the disparate objects—a feather, a lead plumb; man and woman; the quick and the dead—readying himself to release and record their fall.

. . .

WHEN OUR FRIENDSHIP ENDED, JACKIE'S AND MINE, I TRIED TO FIND other women friends. It occurred to me how narrow I'd been for those five years, needing only Jackie's wry, warm company. Or was it depth? How does one estimate the heft of something let go?

I telephoned all the women in my address book. I had dinner with a female colleague, enduring three tiresome hours of departmental politics; went to a few art films with a journalist I knew—a brassy, self-involved New Yorker whose wit turned out to be more corrosive than comic. I spend an evening over drinks with a woman I'd met in graduate school, a psychologist, listening to her confess her wide assortment of disdain for clients and ex-lovers. I met a bohemian silk-screener in her sixties at a party who, before the evening was out, invited me home to her apartment with her hand on my thigh.

I looked up previous women friends with whom I'd fallen out of touch: Lynda, my tennis partner from California, now teaching in the medical school at Yale. We got drunk at a seafood restaurant in Niantic and talked about her fear of growing old. I drove to see my old best friend from grade school, who'd cut off her beautiful hair and become a critic of postcolonial literature. We discussed Edward Said and her disillusion with the past.

Jackie was gone. The woman who'd been my friend had departed completely, even from the vestige of herself. She still looked the same when I snuck glances at her across a room or in committee, but in her eyes, her face, something, a light, an alertness, a connection—had fizzled and gone out. It was like looking for a missing part, a phantom, something that ached but was no longer there.

. . .

WHAT J.-B. PLONGEUR'S FALL BROUGHT ABOUT DECADES LATER, IN NAPO-leon's effort to ease the press of cemetery space, was the formation of several large graveyards outside of the city. Among these was Père Lachaise, the now-famous necropolis some wag once dubbed "the grandest address in Paris." It is a beautiful spot, built high on the hill of what once was a bishop's vineyard, then a Jesuit retreat, then an opulent estate named Mont Louis, with a panoramic view of the city (now rather lost on its residents) that stretches past a tapestry of spires and slate roofs, railway arteries and office buildings, to the green hills far beyond. Plane trees mark the silent avenues that curve around the promontory's verdant landscaping; azaleas and hosta, green-black cypress, and the thorny gold of gorse are massed among the crowded tombs, their roots slowly entangling in the hair of the dead.

The living flock here too. College kids arrive by tour bus and scatter to hunt for Jim Morrison's grave; the literati pause above the tombs of Gertrude Stein, Balzac, or Oscar Wilde, looking a little disappointed, as if they hadn't really expected their pilgrimage to end in front of a wet ingot of granite on a cold spring day. Music lovers, more philosophical than readers, stroll contentedly past the bowers of Bizet and Cherubini, past Edith Piaf's unadorned black stone and Isadora Duncan's remains, enshrined fashionably in the Columbarium. Even the graves that no one seems to visit much—the tomb of Karl Marx's daughter, the vault of a president who died in some redhead's arms, crypts of unremembered savants and Egyptologists and Communards—make one realize that we are all voyeurs and voyagers into the foreign country of the dead.

I spent an afternoon in an English language bookstore, succumbing to the temptation of books through a rain-smeared window. Entering the murk from the *bouqinistes* on the *quai*, I passed the owner, an aging Briton with corroded teeth, guarding the door like Cerberus. Inside, I found an inadvertent costume party of college-aged Hemingways, suburban Henry Millers. A generation with guidebooks, one that could not seem to get itself lost. Even the store was a replica of its namesake, not the real thing. There were used copies everywhere—and I don't just mean books.

The ground floor was a boneyard of dingy paperbacks—histories of the Third Reich, macrobiotic cookbooks from the seventies. The next *étage* offered some literature: Wells, a little Kipling, Charles and Mary Lamb. Near the poetry section, someone was sleeping on a tattered divan—faceless, just a length of dirty stovepipe jeans and Keds.

I descended to the basement biography section and spent some time thumbing through histories of Nixon, Goebbels, Douglas Fairbanks. I found a small book about Rachel Carson, the environmentalist who had died of cancer in her fifties, and paged eagerly through excerpts from her generous, classical prose, so out of fashion now. An amazing woman, she once gave back a Guggenheim fellowship because she realized, rebudgeting one year, that she could just get by on royalties after all, and so returned the foundation's money for someone else to use. A true recycler, honorer of other life. Her contemporaries were men like Beebe and White—stylists, craftsmen, all departed. It occurred to me that bookstores, too, house nothing but phantoms—writers living out the Sybil of Cumae's curse: to be immortal but keep on aging.

An elderly woman at the register wrapped my selection in a parcel. "Come again," she said, and, because death and prose were on my mind, for a bizarre second I took her meaning in a ghostly, haunting way.

. . .

WHERE DOES A FALLING AWAY BEGIN? I SUPPOSE I WAS AS MATERNAL AS any little girl when I was small. I had my share of dolls to tow about and bother with my care, though I seemed always to be getting into trouble for feeding their plastic faces too assiduously, or deciding to give them all haircuts with my mother's pinking shears. I didn't think I deserved to be punished for that; it was bad enough that all my dolls from then on looked like GI-Joe.

My mother worked; my sister and I were raised by my grandmother, who stayed home and devised for us an endless assortment of pleasures. Lunches were arranged on our plates in the shape of faces—carrot curl hair, eyes of pimiento-stuffed olive—and the kitchen seemed always to be scented with rising dough and long-simmered sauces, recipes she had smuggled with her from another world, along with her accent and her strange, softly fragrant clothes. I recall her waking me on the morning of my first remembered snowfall, holding me in her arms by the window, where overnight our backyard had been blanketed in diamonds. I was speechless, enchanted. It wasn't the snow, or the fact that she was holding me that I was to remember for so many, many years—it was the shine in her eyes as she gazed at me, a grown person absorbed in a small person's wonder, my Oma's delight in my delight.

I was four years old when she died abruptly, of a heart attack; I think I was too young to understand. All I knew was that my mother, always glamorous in her office suits, now shopped at Bamberger's for housedresses, and stayed home and fixed us ravioli from a can. Things had changed overnight, like waking to a snow-transfigured world. Winter had come and my Oma had slipped away, shedding our family like a coat or a superfluous skin.

I believe we learn how to grieve or not—what to hold onto, what to let go. There were other deaths in my childhood: a young aunt killed in a freak accident, dragged to her death caught on the side mirror of a truck; a girl in my grade school whose whole family had been killed in a car accident over summer vacation; a kid in our neighborhood who broke through lake ice one year and drowned.

These things were hushed, secretive. Grieving was something kept apart, done privately. I recall my mother, pale and vacant, holding in her tears because she thought them weak. And I recall that same impulse rising to harden me after Jackie and I had fought.

Shame is a force that presses the heart out of shape. Why, in that angry decade, did we never reach for each other? How often we passed in hallways, looking coldly ahead, drifted apart like two polarities in social groups, at parties. Ashamed of the pain we'd caused, embarrassed by our own intolerance.

Now death has put a stop to our foolishness, brought us up short in every respect. How I wish these words could reach you, bring to light once more your face that keeps trying to surface in the faces of strangers. A touch as easy as forgiveness, a remembered smile. This way, and this, is how I would have said goodbye.

. . .

IN MEDIEVAL PAINTINGS OF *La Danse Macabre*, DEATH HOLDS A SCYTHE or spear, a shovel or a slat of coffin wood. Sometimes he's shrouded, or garbed as a jester, or naked, worms writhing from orifices and corrupted limbs. He plays the flute or bagpipe, mandolin or drum while he grasps the hair of virgins, the wrists of reluctant queens. Kings and clerics, usurers and saints, doctors, courtiers, and monks—all are lured into the *farandole.* Sycophantic, jeering, Death holds an hourglass beneath a portly abbot's nose, snuffs out the candle of a praying nun; he drives the farmer's horses, steals the merchant's coins and the jurist's baton; he laughs over the bowed backs of the old, leads a child from its mother's lap, climbs a ship's mast in a storm, fastens pearls around a lovely lady's throat. He is seductive, constant, the one true suitor. His is the tune to which the final *pas de deux* is danced.

. . .

MY GRANDFATHER MET DEATH UNDERGROUND, IN A FALLOUT SHELTER IN Mannheim, 1945. He'd been on his way to work when the air raid sirens went off, so he descended into the closest shelter. A friend of his was there too, sitting across the row, and my grandfather asked the woman next to him, a baker's wife, whether she would switch seats to let him sit with his pal.

They were about to close the doors when someone shouted, "Elfriede! Elfriede's still coming!" It was the cleaning girl, running down the street towards the shelter. They could see her braids flying. At that instant the bomb exploded. Elfriede was never found. My grandfather died instantly, blood coming from his mouth and ears, his lungs incinerated by the blast. The baker's wife who traded seats with him is still alive today.

Not long ago, my mother told me I was a lot like him, this father of hers whom I never met. I walk exactly like him; sometimes, she says, when I cross a room she sees him before her again. My temper too is his—sudden, spiking, then as quickly over, no grudges. That, and my vagrant generosity. When I was a child, my mother recalls, shaking her head, she'd have to scold me daily to keep me from giving away my pens and pencils, toys, hair clips, pocket change. Like my grandfather, who also gave away everything—in the end, even his life.

My grandfather was an anti-Nazi agitator, worked clandestinely with a small printing press, distributed fliers in the factory where he was employed, where the Poles and French from labor camps were trucked in, starved bodies picking between the floorboards for crumbs. The Gestapo never completely rousted the Resistance, which in France was called the Underground. Its headquarters were the catacombs of Denfert Rochereau—a labyrinth of skulls and bone-mosaiced tunnels, a sinuous ossuary that winds for miles under the streets of Paris. Whatever cells the S.S. exposed, there were always more.

Famine. Pestilence. War. Now I ride the subway, another Underground, where beneath fluorescent lights the tired Parisians look spectral, dead. Even the girl with lips the shape of a plum, even the child bent over its paper game, its inattentive mother staring wearily, green in the subterranean glow. The grey-skinned worker reading *Le Monde;* the Chinese woman, her face powdered the color of rice; the elderly black man whose hand rests near my seat. I can see the wedding ring on his beautiful, wrinkled finger—gold on ebony—loose now as time has shrunk him under the pressure of loss and promises. And these rows of others we cannot see, strangers with our faces, who have swayed in these same seats on their journey under the soil.

Above us, in daylight, the old are dying, but defiantly. Near the Bois de Bologne I see a gnarled woman sitting with her elderly daughter on a park bench, the daughter stroking her mother's face in the wan spring sun, the green light of emerging chestnut leaves, the old woman with her eyes closed, practicing darkness. I see a woman with swollen feet and thick, sausage-shaped ankles jammed into high, Parisian heels; an old man as pallid as a death's head swaying, having to pause before a curb—but around his neck is tied a magenta scarf, a brilliant standard of carmine red. Death may triumph, but not without resistance.

I venture north to the basilica of Saint-Denis, where bones of light shafting through High Gothic windows seem like time frozen into shards of color, the stripped skeleton of light. Inside, the church is cold but peaceful. Gray ribs of stone soar, cut by shadow and the tint of stained glass. Beneath the rose window, carved columns mark the tombs of France's kings: on each, a skull and crossbones held up by two sphinxes, their lion bodies crouching, claws before them, the heads of women under hieratic Egyptian headdress. As a child, I too had to memorize the riddle ("What walks on four legs in the morning, two at noon, three in the evening?"), but it wasn't the mystery of human age that fascinated me. It was the enigma of the Sphinx herself: composite, dangerous, eternal.

Yesterday, waiting to cross the street near Notre Dame, I noticed an elegant African man in an Armani suit just ahead of me at the curb. Waiting to cross as well, he turned to look to the right down the busy avenue, and I saw that his cheek had been disfigured by three deep scars that ran the length of his face from temple to jaw. What accident had left him that way? I wondered—this beautiful man, his smooth, night-colored skin raked as if by a massive claw. Then he turned to look to his left, and with a shock that turned accident into design, I saw the identical marks on his other cheek—tribal, deliberate, powerful.

How we choose to inoculate ourselves against eternity—with words or wounds, false coin or promises. How we each display it, inside or out: the Sphinx's caress.

· · ·

WE NEVER DID HAVE A CHILD, MY LOVER AND I. TRAVEL, EVENTS, CAREER changes intervened, and having children disappeared out of the garbled conversation that became our life. The topic had been changed to more pressing subjects. There it is.

On my last Saturday, I get off the Métro at Bastille, take the small stairwell up to the elevated train tracks that have been converted to a public park and walkway. I stroll the Promenade Plantée, sit down for a while in the cold sun near a cherry tree, reflecting pools, a bank of ornamental rosemary.

It's good to rest. I ache. This morning my period came on, and

I realize there might not be many more. My mother began menopause quite young, at forty-six; at forty-four now, my own cycles are getting odder, unpredictable. Still, I will miss them when they're gone. A bit of life goes out of you when you can no longer make life.

I am aging the way my mother's body aged, in more ways than this. I gaze at my hands—a little wrinkled, flecked with early age spots—and even their shape seems to be changing to more resemble hers. I have her eyes, the worried look that sets in sometimes without my knowing; fine ghostly lines around my mouth and chin that I fear will make me look censorious in my later years, a scold, an old hen. In the mirror I see a woman carrying two selves—the young, the old, one hardening over the other like a thickening bark.

I rise and walk again, turn off the landscaped pathway, descend into an underpass. The promenade ends at the roar of the Périphérique, and a side street leads me past littered basketball courts and public housing, then down a leafy neighborhood where institutes are tucked behind high walls and winding driveways.

The museum I am looking for is at the end of a quiet street that deltas suddenly into the busy intersection across from the public gardens of the Bois de Vincennes. Over the portal, a huge fresco depicts hieratic human figures and exotic fauna—the Museum of African and Oceanic Art, last on my list, this mausoleum of French colonialism.

It is cool and cavernous inside. In the Australasian wing, Aboriginal paintings from Pintupi, Kintoval, the Central Desert depict dreamtime figures rising from the soil—vivid, scintillating. *Dream of the Lives of Serpents, Dream of Two Men, Dream of a Ceremonial Pot*: the earth caught on these canvases is animated, pointillist, vibrant with color.

In the gallery given over to Polynesia, gigantic standing figures from the Vanuatu Islands create a shadowy Stonehenge of forms. They are the felled trunks of vast trees, hollowed and carved into drums, silent now. One, the hunched shape of a man with a soaring bird emanating from his head, seems like an island Atlas struggling under the unbearable weight of freedom. A composite figure formed of pain and flight.

Down the hallways of the African wing I find fecundity dolls, *Akua Ba,* from Ghana and Senegal; from the Makondi tribe in Tanzania an abdominal "mask" in the shape of a pregnant belly and full breasts. To be worn . . . by whom? Can one assume fertility, put on and shed the life-giving body like a skin?

Masks of all kinds are invocations of a spirit—whether trickster or demon, clown or god. I stare through glass at ceremonial masks from Nigeria, Ogoni and Anang, black wood, empty eyes, carved lips pursed in an enigmatic smile: the Sphinx's gaze. Eye slits through which nothing and everything peers—vacancy and eternity, the huge ennui and peace of the inevitable. One mask in particular draws me: an Igbo *mmwo,* the stark white mask of a virgin. Death and the Maiden. It is delicate, its features almost those of a child asleep, its ashen lines intended to receive the spirit of a young girl returned from the dead. Like Kora in Hades. Persephone.

A trick of the season or light, and ghostly beings shudder into momentary life, glimmering behind the shadowy eye slits. The white mask becomes a mirror. In its inner darkness I see forms: The woman I will be. The girl I was. The child in her grandmother's arms. And other women rise and peer out, women who were seduced by death too soon. My friend. My young, forgotten aunt. A princess in a limousine. A queen bowing to cross a prison threshold. I think of death's dance, haunting us like the ruined girls and *travelos* haunt the doorways near the Moulin Rouge, their voices beckoning from the shadows of peep-show palaces and stairwells, urging us to *come, come,* whispering that life is a curable disease. And all those others— ghost children, loveless, countless, unnamed; lives missed, friends unmet, loves lost—surface for a moment in the mask's dark lake and drift on.

Who can predict the shape of our trajectory? We are held over darkness and released, tracing through space the edicts of gravity and descent. And yet there must be pattern here, something to gauge, something to give these random fragments weight.

When I close my eyes I see a child beside me in a garden. She is looking at something in her hand, something that's come up from the dark ground. From where I am, I cannot tell if what she's holding is a bone or a jewel. All I see is her head bent in concentration, her hair so blonde and fine that the sun lifts and inspects strands of it like some glowing discovery—*What's this?*—then gathers it into its own encompassing brightness.

. . .

WE NEVER LAND WHERE IT WAS WE MEANT TO LAND. PACKING MY FILES and laundry and a few odd souvenirs, I realize how little I have to show for my time here. A few papers, a few scribbled notes—trying, like Beckett but less successfully, to leave a stain upon the silence. I read the books I brought, am leaving most behind. Rachel Carson is staying in Paris, though I can tell you now that I will never find that book again, and months later, writing this, will rage to quote her and will have forgotten all her words.

Last night, spending my last traveler's checks, I went to a concert in Sainte-Chapelle, under a sky scowling with rain. It was cold in the church—the sopranos wore scarves—but once begun, the sweet, ascendant chords of Bach's *Passion of St. John* pierced the gloom like a sword of fire. Afterwards, I walked out onto the Isle Saint-Louis and leaned over the river wall to where the Seine, swollen and chocolate-colored from a month of rain, raced beneath me carrying debris and treasure.

Strange how we never arrive where we intended; how what we leave behind turns up, turns out to have preceded us. In the distance, the evening sky rumbled, pumice-colored, threatening another storm. But in the interval, people kept strolling, eating ices from Berthillon, lovers leaning against the stone break, gazing at each other or at the romantic buttresses of Notre Dame. I think of us all as airborne—borne up by air and born of air, ephemeral, suspended, creatures of a day. But there is consolation in the fact of flight, and laws as measureless as they are wondrous to mark our fall.

—

The Recovery of Things

1. ANYTHING

WHEN YOU CAME DOWN TO IT, MY MOTHER ALWAYS TOOK THE SIDE OF things. She'd forget to take us children in for rubella shots, but she'd remember an umbrella she'd left on a bus in Chicago in 1961. The recollection of it still rendered her inconsolable.

I guess she figured people could look out for themselves, but things—things were always getting lost and never turning up again. As if once out of circulation, they couldn't find their way back by themselves into the evasive loop of use.

I thought of the dolls' heads that would wash up under the boardwalk at Asbury Park, the lengths of string, underpant elastic, plastic cup bottoms, tennis socks. Things from ocean's limbo coming back as enigmatic bits of trash. Nothings, no-things.

When the wave took me I must have been about five, and I remember standing near the shoreline looking down at my feet under water: two toeless, refracted blobs of dough on rubbery sea-stalks. Then the light was all green, and my body turning in the water's long soft suck, the huge green tongue of the sea moving over me, tasting, testing.

. . .

IN THE CAR ON THE WAY TO THE JERSEY SHORE, MY SISTER AND I WOULD play a game.

"If you could come back as anything, what would it be?"

Fox cub, racehorse, baby whale. Along the roadside, the dirt under the scrub pines would begin to mix with white sand as we approached the beach. *A dolphin. A gazelle.* My father told us that sand came from rocks, that beaches were nothing but huge piles of eroded land. *The McMurtry's dog. A flea on the McMurtry's dog. A microbe on the flea.* It seemed strange to me that the fresh white talc along the edges of the earth stood for the remains of something, was a thing worn down and dead, and not the happy harbinger of summer, the white spoor that signaled we were getting close.

"If I could come back as anything, I'd come back as God."

"Shut up. You're so dumb you'd come back as a rock."

"*You're* so dumb you'd come back as a roll of toilet paper."

"*You'd* come back as Christina Fenucci's underpants." Christina Fenucci was our babysitter, a fast girl of sixteen who teased her hair so high it looked like she'd just gotten out of electroshock.

"Shut up."

"*You* shut up."

"You're so dumb—"

"You're so dumb you'd probably forget and come back as yourself."

. . .

LAST YEAR, THE MAN I WAS WITH AND I WENT ON VACATION TO LAKE Como with friends, a couple approaching their twenty-fifth wedding anniversary. They had broken up and reunited so often in that time that the air between them seemed thick as scar tissue. During the whole trip, they never touched. I wondered whether each time they ventured back together they truly meant to be new people, more loyal spouses, to try again, to come back better. Or was it each infidelity that promised them the hope of becoming someone else, the desire to try life all over again?

I would run in the early mornings on the road that curved like silver piping along the lake's shore. Near Bellagio there was a hospital for the lame, and in the still dawn light the nuns would take the cripples out for exercise on the beach, piloting them slowly, gently touching an elbow or holding a gnarled hand, their habits pinned up to their knees so they too could feel the cool surf on their toes. Near them, a lone bodybuilder out for his morning's worship took his physique to the water's edge and, without a ripple, cut the glassy lake's surface.

The man I was with swam like that. In the afternoons we would wander down to the small pier near our hotel, and he would stand for a moment examining the hills in the distance, blue as a new bruise. Then he would enter the water smoothly, without looking back, and begin to swim—striking out, as he did in most things, alone and with graceful self-sufficiency. He left another life for me, yet sometimes I felt that the moment I had turned to grasp him, he had disappeared through my arms like smoke. I remember the look of his head, varnished by the waves, taking the lake like a bobbin stitching a rippling blue fabric, dipping and rising rhythmically, growing smaller.

. . .

WHEN WORD CAME THAT A BARGE HAD BROKEN UP ON THE RHINE IN that winter of 1943, my mother, they said, put on her swimsuit in the freezing dark and dove into that numbing current to drag back a crate of candle tallow they ended up cooking with like grease. Maybe the war explained my mother's attachment to things.

I can imagine her at that age—pert, pinup-pretty—looting under searchlights. There's a photograph of us on the beach near Cape May, worlds and lives later, my mother sitting on a blanket with my sister and me, just toddlers. She is tanned, made up, with her permanent wave and starlet smile, holding us by the arms. But our faces are inexplicable figure eights of tearfulness, our fingers splayed, squirming. I have a straw sombrero halfway off my head, like a dwarf Mexican bandit, a cartoon of misery. But my mother seems oblivious. She is smiling broadly for the camera, and she is holding us so tightly you can see where her fingers leave white dots.

When the wave took me, it lifted me gently, held me up so softly in its curled dark fist. I remember opening my eyes underwater and seeing a wall of green glass between me and the day, a substance like amber in which all sorts of things were suspended—fronds of kelp, a child's shoe, my mother's umbrella, bits of shell and cork, and me—waiting to be deposited again as something else. *A dolphin, a jellyfish, a whale.* The big palm of water nestled me for what seemed a long time before it turned and, with the force of disdain, slammed me against the churning sand so that I tasted the blood in my mouth, gave me back to the hard world.

No one had seen anything. I threw up seawater like a puppy and got to my feet. Up on the beach my mother was reading her magazines, my father dozing beside her. Everything was the same and everything was changed. My sister was right: I had gone and come back as myself. But it was something anyway, to be staggering up that beach on rubber legs, happy as anything to be back.

2. INVESTMENTS

MY CATHOLIC, IMMIGRANT MOTHER BELIEVED IT WAS A SIN TO BUY ANY-thing new—let alone anything fine—for children, so twice a year, when the St. Vincent de Paul clothing drives had rounded up the flotsam of middle-class closets and the remaindered loot of other people's badly chosen Christmas gifts, she would take my sister and me down to see about clothing at Vanyka's. Vanyka was a volunteer for the St. Vincent Society, and it fell to her to take the used clothes home to wash and mend and button onto hangers before the med-ical-looking blue and white truck came to haul them off to local stores. The piles of clothes in Vanyka's brown, airless living room looked like the aftermath of a war whose casualties surrendered empty sleeves and displayed wounds of ripped hems and gaping zip-pers. Despite the overburdened grumble of the Maytag, the smell there lingered long after on our skin and in our hair—a smell of wet wool, basement mold, and dirt—the sort of musty tang only a pile of discarded clothing can emit. Go into a consignment store and stand deep among the racks of worn, dim sweatshirts, hirsute jackets, and flare-collared nylon shirts and you'll smell it: a puckering rankness, the odor of human heat and soured lives and stale, abraded fabric.

For us, too, it was the smell of humiliation. We knew it as a foretaste of mornings at the school bus stop, where the other girls—the girls from upriver private schools with their crisp tartan-plaid uniforms—would make fun of my sister's and my outdated blouses laundered to ghostly pastels, their patterns so faded it looked like we were wearing our shirts turned inside out. Skirts whose hems were too long or too wide or too crooked; I remember one bell-shaped red skirt I was made to wear that must have belonged to some greaser's girlfriend years before. It smacked of ponytails and Buster Browns and the vinyl of diners, 33-rpm LPs, and the back seats of cars. Putting it on one morning, I discovered a dark stain on the seat of the skirt and wondered how another girl's shame could be passed off and worn by me, as if our secret humiliations were a mantle or a fool's crown, or simply a fashion that the smart, rich girls slipped out of like a skin.

My mother had lost everything in the war, but in her case it had made her hard. She was sixteen the day she learned her father had been killed during an air raid. She had just bought her first fur coat on the black market, a Russian mink found sewed into the upholstery of a sofa that had belonged to wealthy Viennese. She remembers stroking the soft fur of the sleeve, over and over, as if she could comfort her own orphaned self through the coat's borrowed skin. Later, she toughened, learned to use candle tallow for lipstick, sew and resew the elastic of her dwindling lingerie. When there were no nylons, she would draw a line up the back of her naked legs to look like stocking seams.

So my mother was adamant during these sessions at Vanyka's, impervious to our low whines, sometimes our tears. She set her face like an Easter Island icon and stood us up in our undershirts in the brown living room, turning us with hard hands, selecting, buttoning, tugging seams straight, yanking down cuffs as if she could lengthen the shrunk cotton or shorten the knobby, growing pubescent arms of her impossible daughters. Vanyka stood by, with her kind Estonian face shaped like a bread pudding, and behind her, her husband Libor peered from the shadows through his wire-framed jeweler's glasses, as thick as the bottoms of two highball tumblers.

He was the shiest man I'd ever known, then or since. He looked like one of those faded, finely-strung intellectuals who were victims of the Nazis—which indeed he was—the kind of man too easily made grist by the blunt wheel of politics and history. But his eyes behind that shyness were remarkably sensitive and alert, almost like those of forest gorillas who peer out from their jungle of circumstance with a kind of surprising, poignant philosophy. I think it was my sister who brought something beautiful into Libor's life, into that brown house and its old, trapped smells. Lovely even at eleven, she was already growing into someone with knowledge I couldn't yet guess at, secrets that would in giggling moments darken her look to that of someone I didn't know. Mantled by the shadows, Libor stood motionless by the hour and drank in the white glow of my sister in her underthings.

Maybe what finally happened was inevitable. One day, when my pouting sister had just been zipped into a corduroy jumper whose edges were the color of pekoe tea, Libor stepped from near his jeweler's bench, littered with broken watches and cheap silver-plate chains, and held out to her a small blue velvet box. We craned forward as she opened it to reveal a tiny, perfect ring—exactly like a miniature engagement ring, with her name inside etched in fine spider-print, and a diamond like a baby's dimpled knuckle set into the fat curve of reddish gold. It was a beautiful, an exquisite thing. Made just for her. And of course it was far too valuable, wildly inappropriate. Even Vanyka was mute.

I heard my mother let her breath out between her teeth as she does when she's sizing something up, and I waited for her to reach for and return the box. A long moment passed; I looked up to see the color of her pretty, aging eyes change from sky to steel. In that instant I felt the weight of everything she'd lost herself, everything she'd never had. Now here she was with other people's hand-me-down values, thrust into other people's country. I felt something used, but not quite used up, being passed on, driving her to the mistake she was about to make.

She nudged my sister forward to recite her thanks, as if she were dealing a card from a deck. From behind, I watched my sister step forward toward the shadows. We were still taught to curtsy back then. I saw her hair dip lower over one shoulder—I swear she raised it, too, as she cocked her head coquettishly, even in the fat, crumpling corduroy, and looked up at Libor in a way that froze in my mind forever. It was the way she later looked up at the camera in her graduation picture, beautiful and flat with vanity—the way I would catch her looking at the men she dated, as they turned to the wheels of their Lincolns and Jaguars to drive her off into the evening, or to weekends in the Poconos or Manhattan, from which she'd come back with new coats and stoles and dresses she'd throw into the back of the closet until spring, when she could dispose of them with a satisfaction even keener than the wearing.

Soon, that brown living room had become a long-ago thing. But the smells of the stiff air, the deep accents, my mother's injuries and greed had also turned into the setting for something indelible and many sided: the love of a shy, foreign man for a little girl, mixing in her with the slow, inoculating venom of sadness and history and power.

⌒

Grace

I N ALL MY TIME IN AIRPORTS AND RAILWAY TERMINALS, THE SENTI-
mental junctions of the world, I have seen only one parting that
moved me. It was a July afternoon in northern Italy, at a small train
station, ornate as a wedding cake. Two gay men stood in a pocket of
stillness, formed where the crowd's current divided and eddied
around them. Young fingers parted grey hair, muscled body holding
the lank body firm in an embrace that wandered as if to take in every
limb and hollow of the other. They kissed occasionally, exchanged a
phrase or two, but it was that embrace that drew the eye and arrested
the heart. If it was scandalous, it was the scandal of defiant tenderness, *contra naturam* that the young should love the old this freely and
without compromise. It was like the clean strokes of the swimmer,
that caress—reaching forward for the portion of water he must enter
and occupy next, pulling it towards him, cupping its substantiality,
even as he must move through it and beyond. The loved body is
always, moment by moment, being left behind, like water one parts
and penetrates. So we dance most gracefully through the fluids of
love and time.

. . .

I AM STANDING ON THE DECK OF A FERRY, MOVING NORTHWARD AS IF TO
accelerate the season, from the warm abundance of Indian summer
in the south of France to the perpetual dusk of a British autumn.
The seagulls follow us from the port at Caen, wheeling and gibber-
ing, their elegant, black-tipped span of wings rising on each skirl of

wind. A man beside me, cleaning his camera lenses, says they must be worshipping the boat, like an enormous bird-colored god. I disagree. I think they would like to eat it, and are only contemplating how to get their beaks around such a huge and delectable thing.

I am following the man I love to this grey island, defying a parting whose moment seems premature. Scheherazade-like, I want to continue a conversation begun between us, of words and not of words, that over the weeks together has felt like a deep gear-shifting—as when two people at a party somehow find they have shifted in their talk from pleasantries into intimacies so deep that when they look up to find everyone else gone and their hosts yawning, they have no choice but to move themselves to an all-night diner to continue the talk, hold onto the thread of that beginning, grow red-eyed and eat eggs together at dawn. England is our diner, appropriately steel-countered and spiritually fluorescent, in my mind a land of smeared sunrises and revelation.

What is it I want to reveal to him? He has not had many women, has drifted in solitude for much of his life, like a vessel fragile but clean-lined, deep-keeled. Perhaps I want to tell him what a strange and wild shore he is now approaching, one that may harbor or wreck that buoyant, singular peace. Unlike him, I feel my life rise huge behind me like a frothing wake, churning, peeling back black uncharted waters, the enormous question always having been not how to follow or reverence, but how to get my wheeling, noisy hunger around it all.

· · ·

Twice in our time together he has made me ashamed—once in a dream and once in that life we call real. In my dream, he takes me to a house he is building and wants desperately to show me, as if it were a symbol of himself, of his integrity. It is a construction site, half-built, a huge skeletal structure with a lovely view on all sides—mountains, sky, pines. There is a party going on amid the bare rafters and beams: elegant people on patio chairs and tuxedoed waiters. I wander through the open floor plan of the house, and as I drift, I am aware that I am wonderfully, coolly, radiantly naked. I move among the clothed guests, free, feeling the soft air on my skin. At the far side of the house I catch sight of a cliff, a ridge on the distant mountain. It compels me and I study it, tracing its ascent in my mind. But in the middle of my reverie, he comes up beside me with a cloak, attempting to fasten it around me, saying "put this on, you're getting cold." His tone is what is chilling, falsely solicitous. I turn to him and know it is a lie: he is simply concerned about what his guests might think about a naked woman in their midst. I push him off, struggling against the shame he wants to drape me with, saying angrily, "Why do you call attention to what is natural in me?"

The second time was perhaps no more or less his fault than were his actions in the dream. We were discussing a man I'd known for twenty years whose love I felt might now be going wrong. It was hard to talk about because it was so important to me. It was a story I felt would have to be talked again and again to get at truly, yet I wanted my lover to hear and know it. His questions were quiet and probing. He listened, responded with an almost palpable care. We were lying in bed, in a cabin on the lip of an island in a dark, northern sea, and the pinprick of our bedroom light felt indescribably small against the starless night that pressed like a tide against the window. I was listening to his comments, not just as they came through his voice, but in the alertness of his body, the feel of his thigh tensing against mine, the brush of his forearm—and suddenly I had the feeling that he was not so much trying to understand as to dismantle something, like a reasonable husband might try to dismantle the one-time infidelity of a wife he still wanted to go on being married to. In that one instant I felt that he was trying to talk something *away*—my need of this man, perhaps, or my own mistakes and illusions, or the gnarled desires of two decades of relationship—and suddenly I felt deeply exposed, as if I should be ashamed of these imperfect intimacies, the errors and struggles of loving and being loved by another. You see, I wasn't talking to entomb that other love or renounce it, but in order to find a way to reanimate and move it forward, and somehow, lying in bed, feeling the perfect fit of my head valleyed against my lover's shoulder, I felt it was of *that* desire that I should be most ashamed.

How easily the phrase "being true" splits into paradox: between being loyal and being honest. How difficult revelation when one must choose between telling facts and telling truths. Fact: I made love to such-and-such a man at one time. Truth: His body was lean and white as stripped beech wood, and his black hair smelled like the sea. Fact: I am not sleeping with him anymore. Truth: The feel of his sex between my legs is inerasable, rises inseparable from the abundance I bring to my lover now when he touches and draws me, taut and arcing with pleasure like a bow.

Still, I fear that when I tell him about others, his eyes might at some point darken with hurt. I will stand before him, and he will pass judgment on my life as some calculated traffic in hearts, faithless and impure. About impurity he may be right. Nothing is that clean. I look down at his loved body, the gold and white of him that shakes my heart, and know that every kiss is somewhat of a leaving, every fidelity between us something of a lie. And yet we caress and promise and unveil our coded honesties, our complicated truths. The bedroom light does hold the dark outside.

· · ·

IF SHAME WERE A GOD, WOULD ICONS DEPICT HIM CONCEALING OR revealing his face? Would his visage be grotesque or gorgeous, or would it merely mirror back bland normalcy, the enigma of ourselves and our imagined horrors?

I knew a man once, a psychologist whose specialty was helping trauma patients recover from disfiguring wounds. He spoke to me of a client he had had, a dancer whose face had been crushed when her sports car tripped on an embankment, throwing her into the freeway guardrail. She had been beautiful, he said (he had seen pictures), but the plastic surgery was a botched job. It had taken thirty hours altogether to reconstruct the glass-like bones of her face from sections of her ribs. On the last day they were to meet in therapy, she offered him an unusual gift. Lowering the shades in his office, she slipped off her dress, her nylons, her lingerie and danced for him in that small and sterile office, wordless and naked, holding a veil over her face to make her scars invisible, moving for his gaze only the parts of her body that remained whole. It was a breakthrough, like a celebration, he recalled, albeit sad. "Lovely," he said, "the way she offered me the beauty in her that remained."

For a moment he was silent, savoring the ghostly erotics of that encounter. Then I told a story of my own.

It was the summer I'd undergone breast surgery—a rushed, frightening operation, but whose outcome was benign. When the pressure bandages came off, I moved into a friend's vacant apartment in the city to heal, away from the well-meaning but overbearing sympathy of friends. Although one fear was past, I was still too swollen for the surgeons to tell whether the operation would leave my breast misshapen. We would simply have to see.

I couldn't exercise during those days, but I spent time sitting in the park watching the runners sprint along the sawdust oval of the track. One afternoon a young man on his fifth lap stopped, sat down with me, and we began to talk. He was young, not much older than my students, but he had a lively thoughtfulness I liked. When he invited me to dinner at his apartment that night I was pleased to go.

We sat at the folding table in his linoleumed kitchen after the meal, talking offhandedly about books and film. When he asked what brought me to the city, I found myself telling him the truth, easy in his company, laughing slightly at my own anxieties. He listened, watching me with an odd, soft seriousness, then leaned very close to me and whispered, "Let me see."

I must have been so startled, I was motionless until I felt the cool air on my breast, followed his eyes as they left mine and traveled down. The whole side of my chest, from ribcage to shoulder, was still the mangled purple and sick olive green of healing bruises. The sutures on my breast were large and black, like the zippered scars on Frankenstein's cinder-block forehead, and a dark crust of blood had formed around my nipple where the pull of my shirt had made the stitches leak.

When he leaned down and put his lips around the wound, the salt on his tongue stung me like a wasp; the gentlest pressure of his mouth sent an ache of pain as far back as my collarbone. But it was the shame that made me gasp: first the feel of it, then the feel of it burning away like ash as he made love to me with a pitiless tenderness, a clean, uncompromised desire.

I finished my story and looked at the psychologist, hard.

"You should have torn that veil in two. You should have kissed her ruined face. That woman's shame," I said, "was nothing next to yours."

. . .

THE NIGHT MY LOVER AND I FIRST TOUCHED, I WANTED TO TELL HIM that choice is the important thing.

As his hand traveled over my belly for the first time, I could feel the resistance in him. He whispered about fears of inadequacy, explained the need for his body to learn to respond to mine. I knew this was a lie, even though he may have believed it. It was simply that he hadn't yet chosen—instead, he had let his hands fall into this preliminary exploration, his fingers begin an aimless conversation with my skin, as if their own dumb wisdom could bring him to a choice, make some decision for him.

My own body answered his resistance, my desire like an ache held back and cloistered. I knew there was a place in the heart where justifications are manufactured, by which we try to force our circumstances to fit and fill our hungers. I had long since shut down that factory. Now the truth was all I wanted, although my body still shivered and stretched toward its needs, like a cat flexing on the bed beside me, kneading the sheets with retracted claws. The untamed body I live not so much inside of as *with*.

The truth I wanted from him was choice. The act was only a ceremony, beautifully superfluous, a celebration of event, but not the event itself.

The choice is an immersion: the feel of the body penetrating the cold skin of a mountain pool, throbbing in the ache of the water's grip, the current rilling around the waist like iced satin. On the trail, deep in the mountains, he still watches me swim, a little envious perhaps, trying to comprehend what only blood and nerves can know, what only the shock of entry can teach.

As I stand, thigh-deep in water cold as melted sky, he doesn't know that I am forever washing myself clean of that first hesitation, even of the pleasure of his imagined gaze. He knows that I have chosen him, but he is unaware that the choice, even unexpressed, is itself a perfect satisfaction. The certainty of desire is its own completion.

· · ·

WHEN I WAS A CHILD, THE NUNS TRIED TO EXPLAIN TO US THE CONCEPT of falling from grace. It was a perplexing subject, and when we moved on to the Resurrection, everyone forgot about it with relief, except one little girl. The idea of some unplanned, precipitous fall had somehow terrified her, so that for a week she refused to play during recess, as if she expected the pavement to open up under her any moment like cracks in cheesecake. Finally, Sister Hurley took her aside and scolded her with brusque kindness: "You mustn't linger over the negative, dear. God wants you to dwell on the goodness in things."

My lover dwells on the goodness in things. We spent part of a summer in Venice, mornings lounging at a café by the Grand Canal watching the rose-colored stucco of the *palazzi* bloom above the green water. Sun at first soft, then becoming keen as a blade. Sea air caressing. The lap and ripple of canals. Lingering over the various flavors of the city.

One morning we watched a family of tourists at a nearby table—a youngish man and his blonde wife and their little girl, breakfasting on *biscotti* and jam, the child playing with the little cappuccino spoons like doll-house silverware. The spoons and the child's hay-colored hair and the woman's wedding ring glinted in the sunlight, and the man was leaning back casually, reading his paper and bringing his coffee to his lips, slowly, without taking his eyes off the print. They looked quietly content, like a tableau of a perfect Italian summer morning, and my lover smiled as he turned back to me.

At that moment, I saw the man reach out and strike the child. The gesture was quick, private, and familiar, and almost nothing changed in the scene, except the little girl's hands dove into her lap like startled birds and she sat very still, looking at the table edge. The water in the Grand Canal flowed on, the milky morning sun continued to caress, more softly than they deserved, a bank of geraniums the color of cheap lipstick, and my lover was still smiling, unaware of the sudden fissure into which that moment had just vanished.

Yet when I linger over memories of Venice, I remember only being fed by love. Afternoons wandering dim, shaded alleys, a warren of streets, the jewel-box surprise of Santa Maria dei Miracoli— veined marble, cool as a mountain pool, the gloom of holiness a balm to the midday glare. Sweat, touch, and a surfeit of love back in the still, shuttered room overlooking the garden, with its statue of some tranquil saint we nicknamed Sepulchra. I felt walleyed with serenity. Sweetness thick as the moist Adriatic air. The sky cooling, paling to evening. The goodness of things.

One night a week later, back in the mountains, I gave him my life and he let it fall. Confessional, close, touching foreheads over a café table in the dusk, I suddenly opened to him utterly, told him my deepest need. That he love me in my particularity, as no emblem of anything else, no attribution or passion to elevate me. Love me, I said, humanly, without guarantee or conclusion. Then I can be free, knowing this ultimate acceptance, this complete being-known.

Isn't it a shame, he replied wistfully, that women need such permission to live from men.

I felt my heart freeze, my hand pull from his. Something deep gaped, then closed over.

Sitting for a long, numb moment as he continued talking, I realized with what clarity I could hear my own inner voice amid the wash of foreign languages, Italian and German, coming from the tables all around us. His too, I thought icily: an alien tongue, continuing its speech-dance oblivious to what it had just knocked out of its way.

But in Venice, city of pale gold and rose, none of this has happened yet. One moment has not yet followed another in its downward dive. The sky cools, paling to evening, and the shadows deepen in the folds of Saint Sepulchra's vestments, as if she were drawing them close around her against the burnished, lingering light. Behind me my lover is sleeping as I stand against the long window that looks out over the garden, absorbing the stillness, wanting the honeyed light to capture us like amber.

⌣

The Secret Lives of Fish

I wrote my college English placement exam essay on Ted Hughes's poem "Pike," while six hundred miles away my parents were trying to divorce.

An August morning, the room itself like a pond—quiet, airless, light falling in watery sheaves onto silt-colored, Catholic-school linoleum, and onto the uncertain heads of students, undulating in the shallows. *Ready?* the proctor said. Above him a crucifix and a clock—Christ and Chronos—hung ticking against the cinder block like cooling engines. *Begin.* I bent my head, cast off into the gorgeous, terrifying stanzas. My pen scratched peacefully in the dusty light. Across two states, a woman was hurling photographs down from a mantle; a man was shouting words I wasn't far enough away to hear.

. . .

EVERYBODY HAS THIS STORY, OR ONE LIKE IT.

They're young—six or seven—near water, alone. When the fish surfaces, no one else ever sees. It is just there, an aluminum gleam, a skirl of water, fin, eye, belly, and then it's gone.

. . .

TWO WEEKS EARLIER MY COUSIN HAD GOTTEN MARRIED IN ST. LOUIS, IN a gazebo under a sky that glowered with rain. After the ceremony, my sister and I wandered off and stood watching the water boil with carp under the little Japanese bridge in the arboretum gardens. They smelled weather, rose to our two shadows as if we were gods.

They wanted food and we had none, so we threw down pebbles and sequins from our bridesmaid gowns and watched the fish spit them back out like popguns. Their faces seemed exactly formed to register disgust and disappointment. They were fat as loaves, impossibly scarlet, mustachioed . . .

. . .

WHEN MY FRIEND IRENE WAS A NEWLYWED SHE WENT TO LIVE IN Sweden for six months, where her young husband had been offered a research fellowship with Lucent Technologies. One weekend they went boating on a clean, man-made lake near Stockholm with a couple from her husband's office—very polite people, unruffled and blonde, who spoke perfect English and would never dream of letting on how powerful they were in the department, something her husband naturally already knew.

Irene liked the Swedes, and their big, clean country where everything seemed open and on the surface: even the sex in their advertisements felt fresh-air and healthy, and their sandwiches were open-faced so that you could see right away everything that was on them. She liked her husband's two fair-complected colleagues and their cool, Nordic sociability. The idea of boating was fun because it was a little unusual. They had brought fishing poles—not really with the intent to use them—but during a short half-hour when her husband and his two colleagues were discussing radioactive isomers, she decided to lower her line into the lovely blue water. The day was beautiful, the sky as rare and fine as porcelain, and she was newly married and happy, and everything was perfect until she saw the fish with her father's face.

Without warning, the line had given a huge, impolite tug that nearly pulled the boat around at a right angle. The three colleagues stopped talking abruptly and reached for the boat's sides. Irene, startled, wasn't quite sure what to do, so she held on. Her husband was looking at her with dismay; she had somehow begun to disrupt this fine afternoon, and it was important that it go well. The sky was still blue, the couple still neat and politic, but Irene was having trouble just managing the pole, which had made a U-turn into the water and now looked as though it wanted to double right under the boat. She was perspiring and hoped it didn't show.

When the fish came up alongside the gunwale, it had her father's face laminated onto its head. It was the look he'd had at the trial, six years after he'd abandoned them—her mother, her brother, and her— that look of disdainful annoyance, like a stranger who'd just been offended on a street corner. And there was something more—something sly and victorious and horribly honest in its cold, dismissive stare. Helpless, she gazed up at her husband, who appeared to her as clean and foreign as the Swedes. *No*, he was saying, *no. Honey, you can't bring that* thing *into this boat.*

· · ·

THE CARP IN THE ARBORETUM GARDENS THAT WEDDING AFTERNOON had looked like film-noir gangsters, tough but sad. When it started to drizzle they mouthed the raindrops despondently. The bridal party moved under an awning for photographs, my cousin's train trailing her like a sorry tail.

My sister and I leaned over the railing in the rain, feeding each other meaningless baubles. Just words.

She reminded me of the time I thought my father was in love with a woman named Carol. He was always "going to his Carol" in the library, working on a dissertation that never seemed to move ahead. When I got up my nerve and spoke of this, my mother laughed and laughed.

· · ·

AS A CHILD I THOUGHT LANGUAGE MADE A BUBBLE IN WHICH YOU COULD survive. A weightless stillness, a clearing—something, anyway: a wake in the unnamable dark. I was the girl writing alone in the lamplight, unschooled, seizing at something that wouldn't stop leaping, that kept changing shape.

I was always the last to learn: timid, invisible. The summer I turned nine, my father ran his nerves and patience to ribbons trying to teach me how to dive. His face seemed permanently indecipherable, shifting between sternness and exasperation.

I'd stand at the dock's edge for an hour or more, my knees locked, until even my sister grew tired of teasing me and went away; even my father turned to other tasks. *Call us when you're ready.* I was trying to make the mathematics of diving come out right, to calculate trajectory, arc, and entry, but all I got was zero. Beneath me the lake was a world of fish, of death, tangled lines, sinkers, hooks—and the revengeful gills waiting, translucent, moving like the wings of terrible angels in the green and deadly water. I'd seen the fishermen at noon, motionless in their aluminum boats, staring into the black water as if they were looking for their own lost souls.

This I imagined. All I could really see was my own reflected silhouette over the rails, a shimmering black shape against the seared white sky. It was like a dark cutout—the space where I might have been, but where cowardice had made a hole in the shape of me—an emptiness, a shadow. I stared so long that even today I can bring back with absolute precision the fear-leached outline of myself at nine.

. . .

EVERYBODY HAS A STORY LIKE THIS. WHEN IT FIRST SURFACES, NO ONE ever sees.

A poet I know tells me about a time he was fishing alone on the Wapsipinicon River in Iowa, when suddenly a bass so huge he couldn't see past its dorsal fin took his lure for a split second, churned the river's surface like a cauldron, and then disappeared, snapping the forty-pound line as if it were sewing thread. He had been struggling with his own writing, but after that he never wrote another poem. Instead, he married a quiet woman and took a teaching position at a small university where, many years later, he was given a chance at a soul-transforming love, but that got away from him too.

Alone in my room I sketch characters that I myself don't understand: A fourteen-year-old contemplating the blue filigree of her wrist. A battered woman lying on a gurney, laughing when asked what hurts most, and answering, *Hope does.* There is something here that will not stay still. I catch it and it turns, gleams and vanishes, rolling its alien eye back at me, black as an eclipse. I invent a Jungian therapist, clientless and depressed for months, who turns to Schubert and Prozac. He too knows the knife and the gauze. He too knows that sometimes you have to let something go when it's so big you can't see the end of it.

. . .

THE STUDENTS' HEADS GENUFLECT OVER THEIR EXAMS. WORDS RISE, smooth as salvage, murky as isinglass.

> *And indeed they spare nobody.*
> *Two, six pounds each, over two feet long,*
> *High and dry and dead in the willow-herb——*
>
> *One jammed past its gills down the other's gullet . . .*[1]

My father fell silent. My mother's rage had costumed itself finally as desperation. I saw her later standing at lakeside for an hour, thinking it over. I did nothing, went back to my homework.

The proctor trolls the room like a pike himself, young Jesuit wafting past me the acrid smell of celibacy, jaws aflame with acne and suspicion. *Silhouette of submarine delicacy and horror.*[2] The monastery in the poem was a ruin, had always been one, long before the poem began. *Decaying institutions* I wrote, pressing hard on the ballpoint pen to make my mark.

. . .

LAST YEAR, WHEN A MAN CAME UP TO ME IN LINE AT THE DELI AND TOLD me I was the most beautiful woman in Ann Arbor, Michigan, I thought, *here, finally, is someone worth getting to know.* It was a Sunday morning in September, with that impossible maize-and-blue light glinting off aspen leaves, and clusters of chrysanthemums waving like cheerleaders' pompons outside the Crazy Wisdom Thrift Shop. I had just left my lover in bed with his cell phone, to pick up bagels and coffee and a Sunday paper. Here now, hair still pillow-mussed and teeth unbrushed, breathing in rich odors of prosciutto, Asiago cheese, and just-brewed Kona, wearing a skanky grey and purple tee shirt that read "MSU Crew—XXL," I was being told that I was beautiful.

He was a small man with hair that looked singed. Broken veins ran across his cheeks so that he resembled an Andean mountaineer, and his eyes were quick and sharp as a monkey's. *You don't know who I am,* he'd said, but I did. I'd seen him at the cash register at the book-store where I browsed on Tuesday afternoons through old copies of *Boulevard* and *Granta* and tried not to watch him watching me. I thought he thought I was a shoplifter.

"Let me buy you a coffee," I said. He seemed nervous—really pale in the watery sunlight as we stepped outside to the picnic tables. I felt gregarious and warm, newly risen, newly discovered, just born, and filled with love. We sat down with our coffees, and sparrows landed around us like small brown angels.

"My name is Kyle," he said, "and I'm an alcoholic. I think it's important to say that right up front, don't you?"

The warmth in my heart formed a little skin, like cooling milk.

"Did you hear on the news this morning that they've managed to teach gorillas how to talk? I'm writing a story about a carp that lives forever. Did you know the Chinese think carps bring longevity? There's a lot we don't know about animals, or about long life for that matter. My daddy was an alcoholic too. It killed him. Who was that writer who said what suicides manage in minutes, drunks take decades to accomplish? I haven't had a drink in three months. Well, not in two months and eighteen days."

I looked across the street and thought I saw someone I knew. I felt like calling out, but didn't. Suddenly I was very unsure of what I was doing.

"Listen," he said, "would you like to buy a raffle ticket? My AA chapter. You don't have to be present to win. Just put your phone number on the top of the stub. I can tell you're a gambler. Pretty lady like you."

I took the pen he held out. I wrote down a number. I did hesitate before we finished our coffees and shook hands. All this time I had said nothing. He told me he'd see me around.

I don't know why I went back to the bookstore a week later. I was with a colleague, who was talking about the net of language, about discourse theory and Norman Podhoretz. She would have been insufferable, except she was on my tenure committee and I knew for a fact that her husband was having an affair with a secretary in Social Sciences. You can deal with certain people—the powerful, the favored—better if you know bad things about them.

I know he saw us. I watched him speak quickly to a passing clerk, then leave his spot behind the cash register. He looked around for a moment or two as if he'd lost something. Then I saw him run out the service entrance at the back—anything, anywhere to avoid me.

. . .

AT NIGHT, IN BED, I LISTENED TO LOVE'S OCTAVES, FURY AND GRIEF. Storms swelled in the belly of that house while I tossed, leaving in the morning only a signature of limbs on white sheets.

Twenty years later I grade the essays written by other children whose adulthood is still too long in the sleeves. Healthy and self-referential as integers, they are baffled by compassion. I've seen them negotiate the schoolyard, sinuous as young raptors, designating prey. It soothes them to be cruel.

One black boy stays behind and we go over his paper. *I think this is a poem about looking hard at something horrorble that scares you but that at the same time you need to.* "That's not bad," I say. "What do you make of the rainbows at the end?"

Monday morning he's nothing but an empty seat. The secretary stops me in the hall. *Did you know Marlin was a junkie? You couldn't have helped him. Nobody can now.*

. . .

GOING UNDER. FOR FIVE AFTERNOONS I STARED FROZEN AT THE WATER while my father praised me impatiently. Finally I walked to the end of the dock and simply let myself fall off, stepped into the outline of my own absence. The lake came up and smacked me like a big open palm. I wasn't prepared for the sting; I thought it would peel open softly and quietly take me in. The sounds underwater were alien too—bubbles rushing past my ears; then dimly from above I could hear my father shouting, far away, as if from a country whose language I couldn't understand.

⌣

Theft and Loss

I USED TO LOSE THINGS A LOT WHEN I WAS A KID: KEYS, BOOKS, HAIR barrettes, cardigans, umbrellas. From the time I left the house in the morning—face clean, braids squeaky-tight, supplies and sandwiches crammed into my book bag—it was as if the day conspired to undo me. By the time I got to school, my lunch would have disappeared, pens be lost, a new set of jacks mysteriously gone. My braids would open and my hair ties vanish by the end of every day, my fine, wild hair tangled as if someone had mussed me in my sleep. But the strangest thing was that I had no recollection at all of where these items went—not even a sense of suddenly missing them. There was simply an absence as if that thing had never been, and it was only laboriously, egged on by my mother's dismay, that I could be made to remember that I'd even *had* a pencil box that morning, or been wearing some dime-store locket that now had disappeared into the dust, or a tiled crack in the lavatory floor, or the pocket of another, more attentive girl.

Think, my mother used to say; *think what you* did *with it*. But that was just it: I hadn't *done* anything with it, and so, I believed, it had simply wandered off—feeling, through my neglect, unneeded. As if things had their own sensibilities, and might, like animals or acquaintances, casually move on when they felt they were no longer wanted. *Think*, my mother would say, pushing the word into my face, and she'd hold me by the shoulders as if her gripping me fast could help my mind zero in, could make me locate and recover the lost object, like a psychic working with forensics to find the bodies of girls along roadsides. But it was no use. All I could feel was my mother's exasperation through her fingers; things seemed to *mean* much more to her, a child of war and hunger. Or perhaps she clutched me so tightly because she feared someday I'd lose myself through carelessness, like a notebook or a pair of gloves, as maybe I finally have.

Think. I hear her voice, feel the hurt of her grip on my slack shoulders. And I try, I try.

. . .

THIS IS A STOLEN LANDSCAPE I'M LOOKING AT RIGHT NOW. I AM AT AN artist's colony in upstate New York, and outside my studio window the trees are bare, an eerie absence that happened suddenly just north of the Taconic Hills. November's pewter-colored sky mopes through the branches in broken, grey shards, and the meadow is feathery and brown. A dirt road pulls away from the property, curves into the wood, and is gone.

I arrived early to this estate—six hundred wooded acres, and a renovated barn where a half dozen of us will live and work. The place was somewhere on a continuum between rustic and ramshackle: a few mouse nuggets in the dresser drawers, dead wasps on the windowsill. A small library behind glass cabinet doors, frozen in time at 1985. After showing me the bedrooms, the Director took me up a battered set of wooden stairs, down a dim, resonant hall, and opened the door to "my" studio.

I took a step back in horror. The room was dark as an airport storage compartment, windowless—not even a skylight to break up the menacing sweep of its arched, wood-paneled ceiling. A prehistoric metal desk stood crammed into the corner, with its hospital-green, 1950s office chair on shrieking casters. It was airless, thick with the stench of old paint solvent and incense and the dust that emerged from the shadows as the Director flicked on the room's lone, ice-white fluorescent light.

"I'm sorry," I stammered, "but I don't think that I can work here." Even to my own ears I sounded like an idiot.

"I've never worked in—I mean, without a—a *view*. A window. Natural light?"

I had to step back into the hall, the room was so oppressive.

The Director looked at me with kind concern. "Oh, my," she conceded. There was a pause. "Well, perhaps we can make a switch before the others arrive."

Before I knew it, she had zipped my adhesive nametag off the door, walked down the hall, and exchanged it with another.

"How's this?" she asked, opening the second door.

Light blazed at us like the tunnel in a near-death experience.

"Are you sure this person won't mind?" Stupidly, I looked at the name on the displaced tag and didn't recognize it. But what name had I expected? Thom Gunn? John Irving? And did this person's obscurity make things any less awkward?

"Well, no one really needs to *know*, do they?" she chirped.

"No," I agreed lamely. Why did I feel so ashamed? "Thank you for understanding."

She left to pick up her daughter at a school play, and I closed the door behind me to my new, bright Hell.

Half an hour later I was on the phone to my partner at his office. The others still hadn't arrived from the train station, and the resonant silence of the house was starting to work on me as if I were a character in an Edgar Allen Poe story.

"Oh, take it," he said. "What's the big deal? These things are all arbitrarily assigned anyway."

"I couldn't have stood it, you know. I would have gone crazy in that airless hole."

"Look, it was just luck that that guy got the better studio in the first place, and *your* luck that you arrived early."

"I would have gotten clinically depressed trying to work there.

Even now I get short of breath just thinking of it." *So instead,* a voice inside me whispered, *you wish that on someone else?*

"I have to go. I have a line of students waiting outside my door."

I pouted audibly.

"Honey, just take it. Or just switch it back, but whatever you do—"

"Yes?" I expected some final absolution, some nuanced insight on the situation that I hadn't yet considered.

"—you really should move your stuff in now, before the guy gets there and makes a stink."

. . .

Luck. My mother used to tell us a story about the end of the war. In a park one day, in her hometown of Eppelheim, she saw a girl she'd known at school years before. They sat down together on a bench to catch up on the intervening time, and the girl began tragically to tell my mother what had happened to her during the war—how her whole family had been taken from her. Three brothers had died in the Ardennes, one of pneumonia in camp; her parents had been struck in an air raid over Darmstadt—the house in which they were paying a visit was one of only two buildings that suffered a direct hit. Her cousin from the Harz mountains had died of shrapnel wounds, and another was killed in Russia five days before the fighting ended. Then her Uncle Ottmar had broken his back falling down a cellar in Elend.

It was Uncle Ottmar that made my mother start to laugh. Maybe it was nerves, maybe shock, or fatigue, or just my mother's twisted sense of levity. Sitting on that bench as her classmate continued her litany of loss, my mother—hugging herself helplessly, fingers squirming into her sides—laughed and laughed and laughed until the girl, stunned, got up and walked away.

My mother is not a cruel woman. There *is* something grimly funny about terrible luck, and something vague but equally frightening about the luck that we call good. A man misses a bus by thirty seconds that later crashes, killing everyone on it. How does that make you feel? A woman sells her passage on the *Lusitania*. A serial killer passes up a victim because at the exact moment he turns to follow her, she makes a gesture that reminds him of his aunt in Paoli. Chance? Design? And which is more uncanny to contemplate: the idea that our lives are just a chaos of random moments—benign or infelicitous, but ultimately indifferent? Or the thought that behind the twitches and quirks of fortune lies something patterned, determinate, comprehensible?

But this is not about luck—or if it is, it's about loading the dice. Yet how do we judge our actions in a universe as unpredictable and relative as ours? There's a phenomenon in physics called the Butterfly Effect that seeks to show the random consequences of the slightest variable. It asserts that a single butterfly, moving its wings in Africa, can set in motion a chain of instabilities and events that can result in something as massive as a cyclone off the coast of Florida. In other words, the slightest perturbation can have large, cascading consequences—whether good or bad is pretty much unpredictable.

Is it any less arbitrary that I should have recoiled from that room's darkness, or that the Director had been in the particular mood that she was in? Or that luck would have it I had decided not to have an egg for breakfast on that day, which meant I started off ten minutes earlier, thereby unknowingly avoiding a convoy of trucks outside of Norristown and so saving myself another eight minutes' time, which allowed me to miss an accident on the Garden State Parkway that occurred seventeen minutes after I'd passed, and so on and so forth until—by a sheer domino fall of chances, all precipitated by that uneaten egg—I arrived at my destination forty-eight minutes before the others (whose train was, for a whole other Rube Goldberg network of reasons, delayed in its arrival), thereby letting me see the studios first?

There comes a vanishing point to our own agency. What I'd done was wrong, I knew that—but *how?* And indeed, what *had* I done, except stir my wings and watch the sky darken?

. . .

At dinner that night at the colony, a composer who is studying belly dancing and the lush patterning of Moroccan music tells me that one of my favorite composers, Arvo Pärt—that all of compositional minimalism, for that matter—is boring. "*Anaesthetic* versus aesthetic," she proclaims, and steers the conversation toward her own innovative arrhythmias that break metronomic bounds, heaping and accelerating into an intuitive symphonic rapture before subsiding into what she terms "a vaguely atonal *tristesse.*" Last year the New York Philharmonic performed one of her compositions, and she admits it was a disaster. No one understood the sudden liberation from a communal beat, and instead of the telepathic melodic unity she'd envisioned, the orchestra had degenerated into a wreck of individualism, a cacophony of sound.

Do we need harmony to be imposed, somehow, in order to make a connection we cannot forge ourselves? I eat my burned burrito and think of Pärt, his single pulse of music like cool rain. The man whose studio I stole eyes me all evening. I know he knows. I was sure I saw him look at me intensely when he arrived, at the suspiciously curled edges of our name stickers, at his cavern of a studio, back at me.

The thing is, I like him; he's funny and smart. Talk expands over coffee, and I learn that he's recently broken up with a gay partner of five years. His account of their final Christmas Eve fight is hilarious and heart-wrenching; he's a natural with dialogue. I learn that he lived in India during the seventies; that his father's entire family—Russian Jews—were killed in Dachau. He is the only son of a surviving son, and he himself never went to college. This man just won a Kennedy Center Award for drama, I marvel, but he's reading *The Great Gatsby* for the first time.

Each detail seems to shine more nobly—or is it I who polish each trait until it gleams? Do I need to endow this man with a holy aura in fair trade for a view of fields and woods and light?

That night I can't sleep; I burn, imagining snakes in my bed. When I finally do drift off, I dream of my mother's hands holding me roughly, as if she could shake some lost object from me, the way petty burglars in old TV comedies are turned upside down, and a hail of silverware falls from their trouser cuffs and pockets. Discovery and recovery; something exposed, something redeemed.

. . .

STEALING SOMETHING, WROTE NTOSAKE SHANGE, "DON'T MAKE IT yrs/makes it stolen."[3]

For most of the year I live in Ann Arbor, Michigan, a town whose police force is known for being progressive, efficient, even (on their Canon 12-speed patrol bicycles) eco-friendly. I had occasion to interact with them extensively last year, when my house was robbed over a Thanksgiving weekend. Eventually they caught the guy, and a few weeks later I got a call to come down to the station for what the lieutenant on the phone called a "property viewing."

When I arrived at the small police building, nestled between the fire station and the Hands-On Museum, there were already about fifty people there. Huge coffee urns chortled in the corner next to boxes of crullers and jelly doughnuts; three or four uniformed officers kept bringing in more chairs, but still half the crowd had to stand or lean against tables. It was a strange, motley group—folks in sweatshirts and furs, bow ties and baseball caps. There was an implicit nervousness about being in a police station for whatever reason; people looked around them suspiciously, or with innocent, exaggerated *bonhomie*. Periodically, groups of two or three were taken away—"to the Viewing Room," someone whispered, as if we were mourners at a funeral. The officer in charge announced that it might be a couple of hours before everyone had their turn to identify stolen goods, but he asked that we remain in the room until we were called. "Don't any-body leave town," a young man behind me wisecracked in a William Burroughs voice.

While we waited, we exchanged apocrypha about the burglaries. Someone said that in one house under construction, the guy simply walked in and took the tools. In another house he took his time going through the CD collection, selecting everything by Richie Havens and Tom Petty, leaving all of Dylan and The Band. In one house he drank nearly a fifth of the owner's bourbon. The glass and ice tray were still on the counter when the police came; he didn't seem to care about fingerprints, or about making a speedy exit. Some owners came home to find all their lights on, the curtains open, the front door swinging.

In all, forty-one houses were burglarized. A law student. A con-tractor. A retired basketball coach. A professor of social anthropol-ogy. A software analyst and his family, who had just moved to the area two weeks before. There was only one house in which he had been discovered in the act. The owner, an elderly single man, came home unexpectedly and heard rummaging from a bedroom upstairs. The thief called out that he had a gun and ordered the man to lie face down on the carpet—but the old man, who was for that impor-tant instant either too smart or too stubborn or too hard of hearing to do as he was told, simply stood there looking up the stairwell. The thief in the end didn't push the issue; instead, he leapt from the sec-ond-floor balcony to the back yard and disappeared, leaving foot-prints in the mud that would later help identify him.

I couldn't compete with these stories. When he broke into my house, I was out of town. It was only later I found the snapped win-dow-lock, the snarl of jewelry he'd left—things of mine he didn't want, littered around and balled up into a tangle of meaningless stuff. I was almost as incensed at what he left behind as by what he took: in some weird way, I'd been robbed of the value of both. The usual appliances had disappeared—my VCR was gone, the cords hanging like severed arteries, although he was careful enough to take the user's manual from my bedside table drawer. A pillowcase was missing, as were credit cards and a book of stamps—but he'd left the spare key to my second car, which was parked in the driveway at the time and whose key was lying in plain view right beside those stamps. He chose seventeen first-class postage stamps, but left a $20,000 Miata; it was bizarre, like one of those freak tornadoes that demolishes a house but leaves the china setting on its dining room table intact.

Another hour passed before it was my turn to go in. Nothing could have prepared me for the strangeness of that experience. I was taken to a room the size of a ballroom, with folding convention tables arranged in a large double horseshoe. Spread out on every available surface was the—well, *loot* is the only word that comes to mind—the spoils of this man's burglaries. Eleven months of enterprise folded, tangled, laid out, sealed up in Ziploc bags, stacked, arranged, disposed, presented. It was touchingly pathetic—the sad, cheap nakedness of what had once been people's loved objects, heaped together in an indistinguishable mass: innumerable pieces of costume jewelry, wrist-watches, a medal from a State Fair, peeling silver plate, cubic zirconia rings. The more impersonal appliances were stacked under the tables: televisions, CD players, even an answering machine—which I could imagine still hemorrhaging messages into unlistening space.

A few people moved slowly around the tables as if at a solemn buffet. Uniformed officers accompanied us for security. We couldn't touch anything, even if it was ours. But nothing *was* ours anymore. Everything had changed when it was taken, and now again when placed in this cold, public light. Memories had become memorials, dead and ultimately unrecognizable, here in this room with its prob-ing electric lights, its walls the color of nicotine, its guards. Here, what had been silver when it was worn and held against the heart had turned to nickel and tin; gold rubbed off as green alloy on the hands of those to whom it didn't belong. Above all, it was people's lives laid so bare, and the paucity of their possessions strewn about like mem-ory's corpses on a battlefield.

. . .

DOES LOSS GET PASSED ALONG DOWN GENERATIONS? ARE WE SHAPED in certain ways by the losses of those we've loved?

My mother's father was too old to fight, but that just added to their suspicion. Mannheim, 1939. Her mother gone to visit relatives. She is her papa's Aschenputtel, his little beauty, hair the color of milk. *Maedele, Maedele.* She hears a little girl singing, the front door splintering, voices in the stairwell. Her father running, taping papers inside the toilet bowl. He pulls down his daughter's panties, sits her down. *Be quiet. Don't move. Don't cry.* The door closes.

She sits quietly, counts the spots where plaster has come off the walls in divots. Daylight filters through the star-patterned window making watery shapes on the wall. One of her shoes taps the tiles. She starts on the cracks near the ceiling . . . *einz, zwei* . . . doll-sized rivers winding across a peeling continent. Through the door, her father's voice is a melody played wrong, a fist pounding air. She listens as it vanishes down the stairwell, into the street. Then it is gone.

When the whole house is silent, the street and the sky too, she can hear only her own breath, the *plink* of water in the pipes. She sits on the splintery seat in the stillness, sits and sits and sits with her panties around her feet, as squares of light creep across the floor and the afternoon slides into evening, then into night.

A body in motion tends to stay in motion. *Don't cry,* my mother says. *Don't cry.* One morning, when I was seven, I walked into the kitchen where she was, rubbing my elbow and feeling something warm down my back. When I turned around to pour a glass of juice, she screamed.

It wasn't until they swabbed my head with antiseptic at the clinic that I actually felt the pain; the smelly liquid made my scalp feel like it had been seared on a griddle, and I lurched away from the nurse's gentle hands. Eighteen stitches, each an agony like a star exploding. But I don't even remember falling.

Perhaps the truth lies in relativity. Moments of exceptional density draw everything else towards them, warped by that pull.

"Don't move," my mother kept saying, looking beyond me through the clinic window into the parking lot. "Don't cry."

. . .

"WHAT ARE THOSE PLANTS?" AN ARTIST FROM NEW YORK CITY ASKED yesterday afternoon, and after a long, puzzled moment the Director, who lives here at the colony, realized the young woman was pointing to a field of uncut grass. We are in an alien landscape here; we wear orange when we go for walks, because deer season has started, and there are hunters who stray into private woods. It's strange to be marked, like a target, for protection—strange that to be different is to be safe; to hide our spots, lethal.

Ten days into the residency, I have lunch with a friend in Boston—one of the "outsiders" whom we are forbidden to bring in because the colony is insular, sacred to us six. Art Jail. On a rainy morning I drive three hours to Harvard Square to get away from the ringing silence, the solitude, this maddeningly guilt-ridden sanctuary. My friend, a physician, waves away my concerns. To him, both art and guilt are symptoms of the same moribund self-involvement.

"Why not stop worrying and put it to the guy himself?" he says, picking at his salmon, sensible as someone with a conscience made of meringue. "You tell the guy, 'Look, this has been bothering me—such and such happened, now I'll do whatever you think is fair.' He might tell you it's fine, he's really happy there. You don't know; this might have been the best thing in the world to happen to him."

I sense that butterfly in the Serengeti at it again.

"It's the 'such and such' part—how exactly do I phrase that? I mean, do I say 'I stole your studio'? Or 'Hey, I just stood there and let it happen'? Or maybe 'I just stood there pouting like a prima donna until I *made* it happen'? God, I'm so low I can't even do my own stealing."

He pours me more Chardonnay, and I creatively skirt the issue.
I begin to think up and describe inventive penances—donating funds
to have a window installed in the bad studio ("How much can it cost?
I could write it off in taxes.") Dedicating the window to the guy. I
even dream up the inscription, right there on the spot: *Look inward.*

"Well, that'll work, too." My friend turns away, disappointed,
because face it: confrontation is more exciting than charity. You'd
rather see a Christian *in* a Coliseum than endowing one.

"I need to think about this more," I say lamely. "I should write
about this to try to figure it out."

He laughs. "Can you imagine—" he stops for a moment to flick
a speck of cork from the lip of his glass, "—if you actually used this
guy's misery to get *published*?"

. . .

A BODY IN MOTION TENDS TO STAY IN MOTION.

The bottom line is that I'm too ashamed, too cowardly to do
anything. Two weeks pass, then three. We are dug into our respective
spaces, deep in work. I smell the burn of encaustics from the painter's
studio next door to mine, hear the buzz of the sculptor's electric saw
across the field as he shapes cherry wood into stippled spheres that
look like huge testicles. From the Robbed One's studio I hear—well,
nothing much. A little moving of files. The low sound of Tibetan
bells from his tape player. Is that a good sign?

At the colony I work at a fever-pitch, grudge myself any breaks.
I make myself wait to pour coffee until it's burnt black and the cof-
feemaker clears its throat in a death-rattle. I wait to pee until I have
to go so badly I hop downstairs like Rumpelstiltskin. I *have* this studio, I figure, so I'd better *use* it. The thought of blocking now horrifies
me: it's like survivor's guilt. I take no calls. I'm like Thomas Merton
in his cell in Gethsemani. I don't even put a sweater on when I'm cold.

Of course it's a vicious circle: the more *I* write, the more con-
scious I become of his silence through the wall. Suddenly all the

pages I'm turning out feel less like atonement and more like profiteer-
ing. I realize I'm on the horns of a dilemma here, and understand
that maybe the thing about being in the wrong is that, by definition,
you can't be right.

. . .

HERE'S A STRANGE FACT FOR SOMEONE THIS CONFLICTED: FOR MOST OF
my summers during college I was employed as a teller at various
banks. I liked the work; it was weird and important seeming and carried trace elements of risk—like the gunshot-starred glass that was
pointed out to me on my first day, or the silent alarms you could trip
with your foot if you were being held at gunpoint. In some banks,
we were shown training films on how to spot a bank robber. The
actors in line on the grainy video all wore shorts and Hawaiian shirts
. . . but wait: was it the one with the ski mask and paper bag? They
lectured us on how to hand out marked money, or about the red dye
from exploding canisters in special bank bags. Still, I learned from a
carbuncular Brinks driver named Chet that most bank heists go
unsolved, most robbers do get away.

Apart from the threat of firearms, kidnapping, and death, the
work was fairly dull. We tellers spent most of our afternoons talking
about the sales at Marsh's, or trading zucchini-bread recipes. One day
some joker tried to send a milk shake through the pneumatic tube,
and it was a news item for weeks. We wondered why the guys who
came to the drive-up windows always fell in love with us. Was it the
tinny, efficient voice that sounded like it came from inside an MRI
machine, or the voice of the mother through prenatal uterine walls?
Was it the erotics of handling money, sending the bills—twenties
and fifties—whooshing out like billet-doux on Paolo and Francesca's
infernal winds? We had to be honest in our accounting. We couldn't
date the customers, or even accept tips—like the $50 gift from a
wealthy customer my manager made me redeposit into his account. It
kept us pure, somehow, that scrupulous immunity to love or money.

We were virgins, handmaidens, the untouchable Daughters of Midas behind bulletproof glass.

At the end of one summer, the supervisors at Bank of America said I had management potential; they wanted me to stay for training. By then, protesters were assembling every morning in the lobby; "Bank of America Out of South Africa!" their placards read. The administration had to call in more security, beyond Lieutenant George, the retired traffic cop who usually slept the day away in the cool dark of the safe-deposit vault. The marcher's faces looked so earnest and took us all in with their somber, accusing gaze. Could a whole country leave a red stain on corporate hands?

I quit. I said I couldn't work for a company that financed apartheid, and to prove it I also cut my Shell Oil card in two. I felt very moral, but the fact is, school was starting in two weeks anyway, and I didn't need a job or gas. Not to be outdone in posturing, shortly thereafter Bank of America launched an ad campaign that softened its image as a geopolitical world player. It never withdrew a single dollar in South African investments. Chet the driver was right about most getting away.

· · ·

RECOVERY MEANS TO GET BACK AGAIN. TO BE OR TO HAVE SOMETHING restored. It implies that one loses oneself for a while—whether to drink, illness, addiction, obsession, fanatical belief, breakdown. "A recovering Catholic," I call myself jokingly when anyone asks, suggesting that guilt too is an addictive substance—itself a slightly shameful and damaging indulgence we must toughen ourselves to resist. We should feel guilty about feeling guilty. But I'm not sure of that. I'm not sure that you can murder guilt without injuring judgment.

Recovery. You can recover lost property—a term which is etymologically interesting: to "cover" meaning to possess. Rams cover ewes. The old marital laws of *couverture. Recouvrer.* You would expect instead that property be *dis*-covered, re*deemed* of its value, its worth.

. . .

"YOU HAVE NEVER KNOWN THE MEANING OF LOVE, NEVER, YOU WHO have always drawn all things to the center of your own nothingness."[4] How Merton's self-reproachful diary entry struck home to me, like a secret voice. Why is the truth so often a scourge, a fiery Nessus shirt we try to, but can't throw off?

I have said that my mother wasn't a cruel woman. But losses sometimes stunned her, immobilized her heart. When my grandmother—her mother—died, I was only four years old, and I don't remember much about the funeral. Red flowers. A long Mass, most of which I spent playing with the buttons on my white Sunday gloves.

Afterwards, my mother, sitting under the wall phone in the kitchen, drew me to her, lifted me onto her lap. She smelled strange in her new black crepe, the fabric crinkling against the backs of my legs like dry skin. My patent-leather church shoes dangled against her shins, shiny as two beetles, and it dawned on me with the force of profound coincidence that my mother and I were both wearing black.

When I looked up to tell her, her eyes looked raw, and she was smiling a smile that smelled as strange as her dress. "I've lost my mama," she said, nuzzling softly into my neck, lifting my gloved hand to her cheek. "Who will be my mama now?" She began to rock herself tenderly, holding onto me for balance. "Will you? Will you?" she crooned, and I could feel the brooch on her collar pressing into me hard enough to hurt. I began to wriggle free, squirming slowly at first and then harder, harder.

Did I imagine that the strap of my shoe caught in her hem, and I pitched backwards, felt for the longest duration the sensation again of falling? There are losses so rapid you don't have time to feel—until the nerves loosen, the sliced flesh relaxes around its wound. It is fixed in my mind that I opened my eyes and watched her watching me for a long thoughtful moment before she let me drop.

. . .

To me, Arvo Pärt's music is still like the purest voice of sorrow, of longing: all variations on it are stilled, and its intensity is embodied in repetition alone. It is the redundancy of pain, and yet, too, a kind of distillation of sound and suffering, so that each note becomes sweeter, keener, carves into the waiting silence the sere shape of its own agon and offering.

Because it is, finally, what we offer that restores us—the depth of our feeling, nothing left to check or embellish it, nothing erected to protect ourselves, no complication or unearned nuance. Only the thing itself, allowed in and permitted out of us, until we stand in its searing current at last and are cleaned.

Fewest words are closest to the truth, just as fewest notes are purest. *Show me the man who has forgotten words*, Lao Tzu said. *Him I would like to talk to.* Pärt. Words. Mother. Song. I did nothing in the end. About the studio, I mean.

In the story version of this piece, the character called my mother would be holding me gently; her father would never have been taken, her mother never let grow old and die. Uncle Ottmar would be a great-grandfather, favoring an old sprained ankle from a nasty fall, and I might be managing a bank, since the fictional settings of Pretoria and Johannesburg and the Townships would be homelands and grasslands again—peaceful and uncontested because never stolen.

All we take away in the end is the feeling of being held, or held onto, or let go; we try our best to sanctify and accomplish. But the woods forget. The view never looks back. We are beings that have been left somewhere, dropped into a crack of space and time, and our acts spread randomly through the world like dye in water. But I want to believe that the force that misplaced us will come back for us again, that somewhere it is being shaken, told to *Think* where it saw us last.

Home and Away

Every day is a journey, and the journey itself is home.

—Basho

Last night I dreamt about my house in Michigan. It's a modest house—a white-shingled bungalow with a handspan of picket fence, a skinny arbor caught in the coils of a wisteria that, because of bad soil or botanical obstinacy, has never issued a single bloom. "Publish or perish," I grumble at it each fall as I inflict another vengeful pruning; each spring it offers only a toupee of denser foliage. In my dream I am beneath the old silver maple in my yard, a geezer of a tree that still pushes out a lacework of shade every year, though over the decades ice has brought most of its bigger branches down. I am doing nothing but standing under its canopy of trailing leaves, on the lawn haloed by my lit windows, breathing the rich air of a Midwestern late summer night.

Why I should be dreaming about my house at all is a mystery. A child of immigrants, I have been perplexed by the notion of home, a concept I find at once compelling and elusive. Is it something you discover after a long search, something arrived at, a terminus? Or is home always the place you've left behind, that spot of space and history preserved in the glow of loss, of memory? My relatives called it *Heimat*—homeland—a word implying that one is perpetually not there.

If my parents were wanderers, then so am I. I've chosen a writer's life—peripatetic, ambulatory, indigent and itinerant. For eight months each year I close up my house and travel, often without destination, sometimes with little more luggage than a solid pair of shoes and a laptop. "Gypsy," my friends call me and shake their heads. They're right: whether it's Cannes or Cape May, with the hum of wheels beneath me, I feel at ease.

Perhaps that's why, when I dream of home, I am always on the outside looking in. As if through a window, I gaze at the icons of my own temporary, settled life: in the cabinets, my grandmother's heirloom plates, all but two broken now; the paperbacks from college sagging on homemade shelves; the comfortable sofa in its state of irreplaceable decrepitude. I see the paintings and rugs, the feathers and stones it took me years to collect; the Wassily chair I bought with my first paycheck; the dent in the wall where an ex-lover and I, a little drunk on anniversary Moët, tried to move the fridge. I see these things through glass. I am reverie's exile. In dreams, I haunt my own life like a yearning ghost.

But in reality, I am a saboteur of nostalgia. I wake in the morning, and the house around me feels like nothing more than a snarl, a binding web, an anchor. The raccoons have ripped another hubcap-sized hole into the shed roof, the bathroom plumbing is dripping through the subfloor, the drains have reflux, the mold is creeping, and the whole house is one vast blank check drawing on all my resources. In the cabinets I find nothing but detritus, evidence of my crippling routines—*not* those same plates again, not that old photo album spilling its glissando of snapshots: the hiking trip in southern Ontario, bikes by the James River, *God* not those views one more time. Maybe, like the occupied countries of faded love or childhood, home is also the place we long to leave behind.

The essence of things is impermanence, the Buddhists say. Each fall semester I am tethered to a podium at the university, where outside leaded windows, leaves turn violent orange, and the Goodyear blimp floats like a bulimic angel over the football stadium. I teach the works of other wanderers: Conrad, Lawrence, Joyce. When we get to Joyce's

"Eveline," I look out over rows of students, bored and insensate as crash mannequins, and I ask, "If someone were to pull up in a red Lamborghini and tell you to hop in"—a few stop writing or browsing their chemistry books to look up—"if they said, 'Leave your schoolwork, dump your part-time job and your little life. *Get in . . .*'" One or two smile and roll their eyes; like all the young, they are secret conservatives, faithful to what they know. "Would you do it?" I ask, looking over a sea of bland, bemused faces. "Would you?"

I remember a tornado that passed through my town in 1998—green sky, swirling clouds, the trees' white undersides lashed and bent almost double. Lightning tongued the earth for a while as the front moved in, a strobe of searing flashes, the thunderclaps so loud you could feel them like knuckles against your eardrums. Then the wind began to moan in a dangerous, unnatural way: a roar, a crescendo, the afternoon sky now dark as rubbed charcoal. I heard branches rip free, the strange whistling as the gale lifted roof shingles, housetops being scaled like fish. For an uncanny, exhilarating second I wanted it all to go—the dishtowels and dinnerware, the tired wall art, the toaster oven and *TV Guides*—the whole plush dungeon of domesticity confettied down Main Street, all the matter of my life lifted and scattered like seed from a burst pod of house, like candy from a split piñata. My screens shrieked, my rafters groaned as if to oblige me. But the house held.

Birds nest in the wisteria now, and one summer a colony of yellow jackets moved in that kept my neighbors and their patio party guests hopping. The deck is old and smooth, satined to silver with years of frost and thaw. I like to think that when I'm gone, the house stops and waits for my return—the deck arrested in its weathering, the slant of sun across the hardwood just as I was closing the front door behind me caught and frozen, only regaining its slow eastward motion when I turn the key once more and step across its threshold. There is a part of me too that only grows and lives when I am home, that stops magically inside me when I travel, and waits for that elusive reunion to resume. Strange that there are things to which we are most loyal in the leaving. I close my eyes and again I am standing ankle-deep in the dreaming grass, breathing the musk of tomato leaves and loam and sun's heat leaving cedar, in the languid near-dark that will always smell of yesterday and tomorrow.

. . .

OUTSIDE MY STUDIO WINDOWS IN THE ARID MOUNTAINS OF Southern California, the sky above the valley is gradually lightening like a stretched balloon. I am in residence at an artists' colony just south of Temecula, the conclusion of a long journey along the coast and inland, down the flat brown spine of this Western state. This is a strange, wild landscape: I can see the gnarled black outlines of live oak trees and chaparral, the red leather of manzanita, and on the slope across a small canyon the huge, sluttish beauty of wand-like yucca blooms. A dust-colored lizard darts across the floor, and although it is spring here, the air outside is like blue glass, shatteringly clear and cold.

My new abode, nestled in the Palomar mountains, is a large, one-room studio made of glass and concrete, canvas and wood, called Lake Cottage. It stands in a live oak grove near a water-lily pond, where frogs get up the reed section of a nightly orchestra. There are snakes here, and doves: a balanced Eden. Through the trees my view stretches a hundred miles, maybe more, over the haze-blue patchwork of the Temecula Valley—wineries and thoroughbred farms, mushrooming tract houses and the threads of northern San Diego County freeways—until it disappears into the char of distant mountains.

The cottage itself, oddly enough, is constructed like a ship: its roof is canvas that snaps and cracks in the late afternoon winds that blow up from the valley; it sounds like God's underwear drying on a line. The cabin's midsection is ribbed, like the hull of an ark, and the bed is suspended on cables to imitate, I suppose, the lurch and sway of ocean voyage. It's a bit precious as an architectural metaphor, but

I'm growing fond of it. The noise is restful because impersonal and meaningless. Despite the make-believe motion, I know that we are not on a sea, the mainsail is not about to rip. And although the seasick bed suggests the bounding main, I know that we are not adrift on tides, but bunkered into earth on the side of this mountain, at the solid end of a tire-chewing gravel road. We are fixed and permanent. We are home.

At least that's true for the next six weeks, which is the span of my stay here in this generous, peaceful colony. After that, I clean Lake Cottage, pack up my papers, take down the scraps of art I've tacked up as a vague gesture toward decoration, sweep out the refuse and wood ashes, straighten fresh sheets on the suspended bed, and close the branch-handled door behind me. Then another artist comes and pretends the place is hers.

But for now, the sun is filtering through trees—*my* sun, *my* trees—and I am drinking tea by the large window and reading Basho, contemplating his wanderings five centuries ago: "I'm like a bagworm that's lost its bag," he writes, "a snail without its shell. I've tanned my face in the hot sun of Kisakata at Ou, and bruised my heels on the rough beaches of the northern sea, where tall dunes make walking so hard."[5] Basho studied nonattachment; for ten years he wandered, making rootlessness his doorway into vision.

> *Fifth-month rain—*
> *Poems pasted to the wall, peeled off,*
> *Leave traces.*[6]

It seems he too cleaned cabins when he left.

Part of the reason for my own travel has to do with attachment and its alternatives. I had just ended a long-term relationship in the fall; the man I'd loved for eight years hadn't in the end been able to free himself from the tangles of a former life. What do we stay loyal to, long after it seems to have died? He had been married when we met, and although he divorced within a year—a process he'd already started—he had remained ambivalent and indecisive. Half a decade later, he still resented me for the very thing he had once looked to me for: the reanimating of a static, bloodless life. Guilt can corrode, like acid, or it can harden into an armor, a shell that prevents new growth. For years we had stood looking at each other across a chasm. How did we get here? How did we let things go this far, this wrong? Now, numb with recrimination and tears and finality, I felt like someone had reshaped my heart with a tool press. Mortality has many facets. Losing love at forty-five is one.

I needed to think about these things, and in order to think I needed to be in motion. I consider it a form of pacing on a grand scale, covering counties instead of carpeting. When the colony called to offer me a residency, my bags were already packed, my car just idling to be pointed toward some destination.

Nights in Lake Cottage are dark. There is no electricity here, so I make small pools of brightness with kerosene lamps and candles. They are like holes in the darkness; they don't so much light the room as make the night that's crept inside a little threadbare. Then there's the solitude. The evening winds die down, sunset leaks away, and with the darkness settles a seclusion deeper than the one in daylight, where I at least can escape myself through vistas, books, and rambles. Now the night presses in, and the stars bob on its heavy tide like sea birds. Windows give me back nothing but my own face, staring astonished at itself in candlelight.

"I have only the drip, drip of the spring to relieve my loneliness . . ." Basho wrote. "And when the sun has begun to sink behind the rim of the hills, I sit quietly in the evening waiting for the moon so I may have a shadow for company, or light a lamp and discuss right and wrong with my silhouette."[7]

I too am inclined to debate myself. I have a fantasy of an ethical second self—the one who makes the right choice, who leaves instead of stays on the fatal evening, who instead of indulging in the crash of revelation veers from disclosure and returns to modesty, who neutralizes desire or turns it elsewhere. Where would she be now? Clean-souled, sleeping the night through dreamlessly, waking each morning to stretch in the generous sun like a model in a mattress commercial—the kind who always looks unrumpled and refreshed.

The kind who always sleeps alone.

. . .

I've taken a circuitous route to get here, which included stopping for the Christmas holidays to visit my parents in their retirement resort in Mesa, Arizona, where they spend winters winding down their life after forty-seven years of marriage. It strikes me as strange that my parents have chosen to conclude their lives in a place with so little history, a town so featureless and recently inflicted on the desert landscape that outside its irrigated grid of green, the scenery looks like noon on Mars. But I am contemplating fidelity these days, and from the long-awaited perspective of midlife, my parents are becoming interesting subjects for study.

For five days I followed a dipping winter jet stream into warmer weather, driving through St. Louis, Joplin, Amarillo. Speeding through the Illinois plains in the December dusk, I remember thinking it was the flattest land I'd ever seen, as if someone had poured the horizon from a bucket. A dusting of snow on dilapidated trailers, pickups scabrous with rust, shabby shacks—each with its satellite dish and its chicken-scratch yard. But there was violet light, as beautiful as anything dreamt of by Monet, and crows flying slowly, high and separate in the cold, dense air.

It happens every time I travel. The moment I leave home it begins. My senses reawaken, my vision seems born again, even in the most dismal spaces—some run-down Motel 6 outside of Davenport with rooms that look like crime scenes, a floodlit parking lot in Springfield that stinks of diesel oil and pesticide. It's sudden, sure, works every time—the moment I pull away from home, I wake from the fairy-tale sleep of what I know. I come alive.

There were fields in Missouri as green as Frank Baum's Emerald City in the winter rains, storm clouds swollen with snow over the pavement-colored plains of Oklahoma. And there was sunrise in Amarillo: a smudge of ocher along the horizon, then a blush tinting the clouds—flocks of them, mesas and canyons of cloud, everything brightening into lavender, citrine, amber. On I-40, cars and semis pulled over to watch; truckers with license plates from Indiana and Ontario stood beside their rigs, hands on their hips, watching the sky blaze. Suddenly I noticed that one of the cabs itself was on fire, billows of greasy smoke issuing from the hood, cop cars glittering around it as traffic slowed. Nearby, a Ford Pinto had parked, stuffed to the windshield with clothes and CDs, and its driver, a young woman, had gotten out and was standing near the burning truck, ignoring it, clicking photo after photo of the horizon's wild apocalypse. One minute the sky was eggshell green and the clouds the color of fresh blood; the next, the arroyos were suffused with purple and the air shot gold. We were all of us drop-jawed—cops, truckers, the young camera-toting woman, and me—watching these sublime conflagrations, until eventually we turned back to our vehicles under a lightening sky and headed on.

It was late afternoon on the fifth day when I arrived at my parents' retirement resort. After nearly half a century of marriage, my parents have paid $30,000 for a strip of gravel that backs onto a flash-flood runoff canal and edges together with several hundred other mobile home sites in this desert palisade. The homes are tiny—four hundred square feet is the allowable max—and each shoebox is aggressively personalized to the point where each has its identical set of garden dwarves, its glitter-rock landscaping, its potted miniature lemon tree, and a placard announcing its inhabitants, like nametags at a convention: *The Schnabels, Sig and Marion; Buzz and Edie Cornell; Dolly Z's Hide-A-Way; Whitts' End.* It's December and eighty-two degrees.

Because seasons are invented here, the resort is a spangle of holiday lights, living room windows lit up like slot machines, plastic reindeer on green gravel lawns melting in the nuclear blast of desert sun.

Theirs is one of countless such oases, thrown up in the seventies and boom-time eighties, each with its buoyant, optimistic name: Fountain of the Sun, Palos Verdes, Mirage. You can drive for miles down Mesa's main strip and pass block after block of identical mobile home parks, each unit flickering past like a movie-reel frame, punctuated by the regular vertical lines of forty-foot date palms. Here, the elderly are parceled into lots, their parked homes homogeneous—modest, cheerful, clean—what they themselves would like to be, what they would like to remember of their lives: not the quarrels and the messy drunks, not the bitter children, finances, losses, war—but happy, interchangeable Christmases, birthdays, and graduations, lives well led and orderly, merging into the eventual democracy of death.

My parents are already waiting when I pull up, having coffee with a neighbor whom they've co-opted into recording our reunion. He totters down to the sidewalk like an aging paparazzo to take our photograph: my mother, my father, and me, posed stiffly in front of their decorative agave plant and their new patio furniture, moved so it would fit into the frame—white plastic, upholstery the color of a cocker spaniel's fur. "Just be yourselves!" he shouts, as if we were a quarter mile away. We try. My mother smiles winsomely; my father smoothes his silver hair. Behind us the Arizona sky explodes, lobelia blue, threaded with jet trails.

I stand with a fixed grin, my arms around each of my parents as if I were the link holding these two drifting souls together. My mother's frail, birdlike shoulder rests awkwardly under my palm. My father lists a little, gives my arm a squeeze—half in love, half to steady himself. When did they manage to grow so old? I clutch them both, as if I could batten them down to earth, keep them from floating through my arms like smoke. "Careful of my blouse," my mother mutters through her unmoving smile.

The shutter falls, and like a string snapping, everyone relaxes. We exhale loudly, as if being ourselves had nearly been too much of a strain. I think my ideal photograph would leave our figures out of focus: my parents moving slowly into the haze of old age, me porous, the family itself a puzzle that could break apart at any moment, home an entity that could simply lift up and leave. Perhaps we would be embracing, since that act is so ambiguous, a gesture both of welcome and departure.

. . .

FOR THE NEXT SEVERAL DAYS, I FOLLOW MY PARENTS ON THEIR DAILY routines—my father's morning tennis in the senior league, my mother's yoga. On Sunday, I go with them to church at St. Anne's, where Latino families fill the pews, pass their babies from arm to arm during hymns, and smack their teenagers when they finger their cell phones, bored. Across the street, Christ's cause advances in the Colfax Street Mission Baptist Church of Greater Mesa: the small aluminum-sided building throbs with music, while women go in and out the doors wearing hats the size of topiary. St. Anne's is less boisterous, but it has its own diversions. On the Sunday we attend, my mother is wearing a purple fleece jacket over her dress, because the church is so air-conditioned that even the altar flowers take a month to wilt. A toddler in the row ahead of us squirms in his father's arms, sights my mother, and in delight squeals, *"Barney!"*

My mother has evolved a few eccentric notions about religion. Like the belief that the Catholic Church might now allow priests to marry.

"It's because they can't recruit the young ones," she insists. Over lunch we debate the point to absurdity.

"It's not the NFL, Mother. They don't give out incentives." Neither of us backs down, and we glare at each other over potato salad as if the Council of Trent hung in the balance. My father, fearing dessert might be delayed, tries to make peace.

"I think your mother means in theory. Maybe they marry but stay celibate."

My mother throws him a bent look.

"Like *us*, you mean?"

A Roman Catholic, my mother always labeled marriage a sacrament. *Let no man put us under*, she'd say portentously, in her thick English. My sister and I couldn't begin to imagine what she meant. Baptism, Confirmation, Extreme Unction—all were exotic enough for sanctity. Weddings, too, glamorous as we'd seen them in magazines, or spilling out of St. Paul's Church on Saturdays in June as we'd drive by: a cloud of white tulle and best men in black morning coats. As girls, we couldn't wait to stage our own, imagined the church opening on the glittering event like a fold-out dollhouse whose contents we moved around in endless, alluring configurations.

But marriage was what happened over the breakfast table—my mother still stockaded in huge wire curlers, her face greasy with last night's cold cream, standing at the stove fixing eggs. My father smelling of soap, polishing his shoes from a box that had one wooden footrest and opened to reveal tins of grinning Black Cat shoe polish. There were fights in distant rooms, inanities, flirtations, sadness and silence, propriety, criticism, muted discussions about the future. Toilets flushing before bed.

What god presided over this?

I've spared my parents the knowledge that I fell in love with a man who was married. You'll note I didn't say a "married man," which is a different entity—a cliché, a sordid joke, something to avoid. Married men were what other women fell in love with: desperate men with bank accounts and obligations, men whose hairlines had receded as their waistlines had expanded. Men who wanted one last joust with youth. I'd run across married men before; they were easy to spot, and easier still to skirt. The man pocketing his wedding ring with conspicuous concealment in a corner of the bar; the man I met at a party who nearly followed me home, but veered off down a side street when he heard an ambulance go by, so guilty he thought every siren was for him. No, I fell in love with a man. That man turned out to be married. Moral mileage is a curious commodity. Somehow, eight years ago, I thought the distinction was real.

In the evenings, my mother turns the radio to the Christian soft rock station and brings out silverware. My father lights barbecue briquettes over a small square of AstroTurf behind their shed, puts slabs of meat down carefully on the grill. He limps from his old war wounds; maybe we both do. Above us the evening sky is red as an infection. The clouds look like embers; scarlet leaches into the sky. In a few moments it's gone, as if the color had suddenly drained through some opening in the horizon. The clouds have turned gray, and the edge of the earth is now just a line of orange, then beige, then blue. The palm trees are elegant black silhouettes against the disappearing sky.

· · ·

IN TEMECULA EACH SUNSET SPREADS ITS FLAMING WINGS ACROSS THE sky like Rilke's dreadful angel. Evening happens rapidly here, like most things in the desert's abrupt, alarming landscape—this is wilderness as opposed to home. One *wanders* in a desert, like the ascetics, lost pioneers, or forty-niners, drifting for gold.

Last night at dinner, the artists sat around by candlelight and lantern's glow eating the local fare: *carne asada*, tortillas, cabbage, guacamole, beans. A small feast the caretaker's son cooked up for us. He was a young man who'd vagabonded for years in Mexico and told us stories about the lost souls down there who panned for gold—outlaws and castabouts who, even now in the twenty-first century, drysluiced their way through Baja, hid illegal Geiger counters in their pickups, spent lifetimes roaming for some elusive, distant prize.

"Three months of nothing," Matt said, "then one dude walks in a hundred yards and digs up a nugget worth $10,000." He told us about a guy who prospected right down the road in Temecula Creek, a dry arroyo just east of town. This man would walk barefoot down the stream bed while the townsfolk watched; every so often he'd lift a foot as if he were pulling out a sticker.

"The guy was picking up nuggets with his toes. His neighbors never could catch him. In just over a year he got rich enough to buy a floatplane and move to Alaska."

"No mistaking gold," Matt's father grumbled, like he was describing an enemy. "Heavier than anything else and man, it glitters." One prospector they both knew always kept a vial of nuggets on him. He looked at it every few hours to train his eye; gazed and gazed until his vision was sharpened like the point of a pencil, like a hunting dog's, for one thing only.

"It gets to you. It's an obsession." Matt shook his head. "Gold fever."

We ate some more in silence. Across the table was a young artist from Montana, dreadlocks and violet sunglasses, Ani DiFranco on her Walkman; there was an architect-muralist from the South, a ruddy-faced composer, a Chinese performance artist, a shy story writer from New York. All day we had been staring at our own ideas—our canvases, our scores, our empty pages—composing, revising, training our visions, mesmerized by our own reflections in the glass, by our own vials of gold. Sometimes art, too, strikes me as a less than healthy enterprise.

The party broke up late, and there was a full moon above the mountain, eerie and metallic, like mercury poured over a frozen landscape. We stood for a moment, fragile as a mobile, circling each other, suspended in new relations for an instant, until some inner breeze shifted and we turned away. A few good-nights, then each of us took a different path to our cabin. Each separate roadway gleamed before us—unique, imaginary, endless—like a river of hammered ore.

. . .

WHY IS IT THAT IN ALL MY TRAVELS, I SEEM TO KEEP LOOKING FOR HOME?

I browse the world for a place to perch, imagine myself settling down in a crofter's hut on the Isle of Skye, or transported to some pastoral cottage in the Bavarian Alps. There was a Morvandelle farmhouse in Burgundy that I nearly purchased, a ramshackle stone grange that looked out over frosted January fields and white Charolais cattle and a tiny river called the Dragne. In the end, for reasons lost to me now if I ever had them, I ventured on. For years I shopped for property in Michigan's Upper Peninsula, spent long November evenings sketching the floor plan of my own imaginary Walden on eighty acres, by a lake so huge it boasted its own set of tides. Everywhere I go I have an eye for settlement. I am a claim jumper, a global nomad with a Platinum card.

What is it I am looking for? Peace? Roots? A place to write? A depth I've never found?

For a while, the man I loved and I hunted for real estate together—thinking, perhaps, that a house might make a home, despite a love with so many faults in its foundation. We bickered our way through the patience of three realtors, traipsed through other people's houses with the tenacity of spies. We viewed neighborhoods of identical French colonials that from a distance looked like Arlington with two-story stucco headstones. We stood by strangers' pools in the August heat, the air heavy as a flat tire, staring at the sag of deck chairs formed to the shape of someone else's friends. We looked at living rooms whose walls were painted shades named "Lullaby" and "Rubens' Flesh," stepped lightly over aquamarine shag carpeting.

We did find one house perfect for us. An eighteenth-century millhouse on three acres, with a Euro kitchen and new copper pipes, six fireplaces on three floors, two of them walk-ins. The owners, an elderly couple, loved us, brought the price down to meet our budget; our realtor was excited at the fit. As we walked past the hundred-year-old greenhouse, past the natural slate pool, under blooming arbors, I gripped my lover's arm with pleasure, only to feel him tighten and pull away. His eyes avoided mine; I sensed he had slipped into some maelstrom of memory. After one more pass, he turned to go. Our realtor, startled, made some apologies to the gray-haired couple, and we followed him down the driveway to our cars. After the realtor had driven off and our hosts gone back to the patio that was still theirs, I turned to his stony profile, sick with realization. "We're not going to buy this house or any other, are we?" His silence answered me.

. . .

I MARVEL AT HOW EASILY MY PARENTS LEFT IT ALL BEHIND.

Emigrating from Germany as newlyweds after the war, they shipped out on a Polish freighter with only one handbag apiece, spent their last inflated *Deutschmarks* on frankfurters that my seasick mother ended up sending undigested over the railings. They laugh about it still—leaving it *all* behind.

Even their memories. When I ask about the war, they evade. *That was another time,* my mother says and sets her jaw, as if the past were a door that could simply shut behind you. In a heartbeat I am twelve again, in our car on the way to Kresge's, nagging her to tell me about the Jews. Her eyes slide away, like someone offering condolences at the funeral of a stranger. *It was. Terrible. Of course. Shocking.* Her words are rubbery, inanimate, something inflated to fill a lack.

It's when she speaks of injustices done to her that my mother's voice ignites, her eyes become so hard her look could pound a table. The woman in Kingston, Ontario, who turned them out in the snow because they were German immigrants; the nasty people who employed my grandmother as maid and cook, then fed her nothing but apples for dinner. Our green Dodge floats into the shopping center parking lot, where a profusion of housewives wrestle with bountiful carts. *Is that true?* I ask. She turns away, sullen as a child. *You don't know what it was like. You'll never know these things.*

I asked my mother once what her earliest memory was. She laughed, said it was a Christmas in the Schwartzwald; she might have been three or four. There was a man dressed up like St. Nicolas yelling at the children for being bad. My mother, timid, stood quietly to the side, but Santa singled her out: "You too, little girl. You needn't act so holy. I'm sure you've done something wicked too."

That was 1931. Within ten years the world would learn new words for evil. Leni Riefensthal, filming the Reich's glory, wept when she saw the treatment of the Poles. *Tell me what I am guilty of . . . Tell me. Is it for being born in a certain time?* And Ovid: *"non peccat quaecumque potest"* . . . only a sin professed can render infamous.

On Saturdays at the retirement resort, my parents go ballroom dancing at the recreation center. Couples, some amazingly good, glide around the polished dance floor doing the foxtrot to songs like "Dankeschoen" and "Chattanooga Choo Choo." The women are arrayed in chiffon and sheaths of shiny fabrics; some wear corsages the size of funeral wreaths. The whole room smells of carnations and mothballs.

When she was a girl, my mother and her friends played tennis in the craters left by incendiary bombs, laughing, shouting the scores, surrounded by the blackened shells of buildings. At the end of the war, my father, lost on the pitted roads of the Silesian countryside, rode his motorcycle by accident into a town the Russians had captured and saw the German soldiers—young boys, sixteen years old—they had crucified with nails against the walls of barns.

Gliding in each other's arms now, my parents look elegant and European. Even my father, with his game leg, musters a lubricated grace. They dance on the balls of their feet across this cold, glittering surface, revolving like a toy couple on a game board, and they don't sit down until the music stops, until everyone looks up and applauds.

. . .

WHEN WE WERE CHILDREN, MY FATHER USED TO POSE US A RIDDLE, A kind of parlor game. "If your house were on fire, what object would you save?" Money? Jewelry? Mementos?

"Books," I said one time.

"Idiot," my sister murmured. She upped the ante with "Artwork."

I looked around our living room at the fake Kokoshka in the fifty-pound frame, my mother's yard-sale porcelain spaniels.

"*You're* the idiot," I countered.

Each year as we got older, we tried to finesse the question.

"How *fast* is the house burning?"

"Supposing what you *really* want is packed away?"

We'd try to catch my father out: "Do sleeping people count as objects? Do plants? Do pets?"

"Photographs," I ventured one year. I was fourteen, almost old enough to have a past, but not quite old enough for it to need much saving.

I remember a snapshot of my mother as a baby, a studio photograph that has her lying naked on a white fur rug. She is smiling her elfin smile up at the camera. Outside, the Depression is just a rumor, Hitler still only an angry young agitator. The war has not begun; her parents are not dead; there are no losses yet; all her life is still before her, flat and inscrutable as the photographer's lens. What we capture is not so much the past as the lack of future; it's not the shot we preserve, but the open iris of the shutter, the place where we begin.

After the war, my father got a teaching job on the East Coast, and we cast off on the immigrants' move into the suburbs, into a brave new world of accumulated things calcifying around us like a shell. Our yard grew bigger; each new house had more rooms, more slipcovers on the increasingly expensive furniture; our driveway became littered with bikes and car parts, gardening equipment, barbecues. Just like the other houses in our expanding neighborhood, where sprinklers thwacked on summer nights over newly seeded lawns, and fathers played softball with their gangly, pencil-necked sons who would go on to medical school.

Isn't upward mobility just a voyage like any other? Leaving the familiar land of ethnicity and class—the cooking smells, the accents and rituals—to cross gleaming waters that could buoy or drown you, that try to wash you clean, at any rate, of where you came from.

In my blood are the tides my parents crossed to reach this shore. A child of wanderers, I am forever looking behind me at a place receding from view, forever ahead to some imaginary destination, a point on the map that looks like promise.

. . .

WE THINK THAT WE INHABIT HOUSES, THAT IT IS WE WHO TOUCH DOORS, close cabinets, brush against lintels as we pass—when in fact it is the house that holds us, that strokes us lightly with its planes and edges as we stumble down its hallways in the dark. It is the night-black wall that guides us, the unseen stair that lifts to the footfall, steering the dreamer down to cellars from which to awake in terror, or up into attics filled with stars.

I think home is where time resumes, where the sun on the floor begins to move again. Our travels in the world, though they seem filled with speed and motion, are really just agitations, suspensions from ourselves—wind in our branches, petals on the grass—while real time rests like sap, deep in the root.

My own house is a house of time. I feel so keenly the passage of seasons through it, a thread on which memory is strung like beads. *Passage* is a many-spoked word, radiating into space and time. As if years were hallways; as if the body translated through rooms assumed the poetics of some larger voyage.

The Japanese call it *mujo*—transience, the ephemeral. *As we consider today, it has grown tomorrow. As we consider spring, it has become autumn.* Basho quipped, complaining about his joints, "we all in the end, do we not, live in a phantom dwelling?"[8]

Once, looking at things this way, I suddenly realized that the man I loved had grown old. It was a winter evening, two, maybe three years ago, and I was standing by the large picture window in my house looking at the reflection of the room that the glass threw back. Behind me, Christmas tree lights winked, and my lover was cleaning up in the kitchen. For an instant I barely recognized him—a stooped, shuffling shape, swiping the countertop with infinite slowness. Age reveals itself from within—a creeping something I recognize more and more these days in my own mirror image, an older woman I don't yet know coming through from beneath the familiarity of my features, like the shade of my mother waiting to emerge.

What I saw in the reflection of my lover's stooped back and shambling motions was how heavily his life had begun to sit on him, how the boy in him seemed to have bent at last under the weight of error and dailiness, the ineluctable burden of a worn-down kitchen sponge, the strain of living on the fringes of his past life like a poor relation. I feared sometimes that by offering him life and love, I had upset a fine balance that had kept him afloat. Now I saw him drowning in the reflection of that dark glass, he and I caught together, tangled up with each other under a sheen of green water that had proven impossible to cross.

In my dreams of home, there are also empty rooms, rooms never inhabited, landings paused on, hallways that long ago disappeared into the gloom. Lost years, lost love, the wind that closes doors behind the startled, helpless dreamer. A stairwell wreathed in fog, and from the top, someone I cannot see is calling me.

. . .

MY PARENTS, TOO, SURVIVED AN INFIDELITY—SHUSHED AND UNSPOKEN —my mother's brief passion for a younger man. Nights of tearful phone calls, my father's suitcases and hotel bills, dramas and denouements, as if they were catching the contagion of divorce from this new country. But the storm settled, the house held, and they returned to the habits of love. The door closed on yet another episode— quietly, finally—as it did on so much else that became the past.

I questioned my father once about how they had made their marriage work.

"I asked very little of your mother," he grinned, "and she was just the person to give it."

The joke may be truer than he knows. My mother whispered to me once about a love she'd had before she met my Dad—a beautiful young man from Hamburg. This man had once given her a story by Rabindranath Tagore, an enigmatic tale about a husband who strayed into the brothels of Bombay, dissipated himself there for weeks. Afterwards, the wife in the story loved him so boundlessly she took him back. When people asked her where her man had been, she smiled and answered, "Heaven."

"Would you be human enough to do that for me?" my mother's lover had asked. Note that he said *human,* not saintly. That interested me. He must have known that haloes, like homes, can be tight-fitting things.

It frightened my mother, such boundlessness. Sainthood was easier. Religion had always been her fallback—not rapture or martyrdom, but the divine as a form of security. In her catechism, God was a bit like my father: reliable, on time, a man who kept his promises, who never strayed. A man with no surprises.

She left that wild young man. Married my Dad a few months later. "Nothing comes from nothing," she would say in her homespun way of arguing the existence of God, a phrase that could as easily be turned like a mirror on all our hearts—their fear of risk, their need to encompass, even if that means diminishing. Nothing from nothing.

But something does come, if not from nothing, then from Nothingness: no-thing, the not-self of what is large and uncontained. It's the space we try to frame in the windows of our homes, the fire we attempt to imprison in our hearths. Passion. Wilderness. Forces unhoused.

Six months after my mother's marriage, she received a postcard. On it were two lines of poetry: *So floge meine Seele / Als floge sie nach Haus.*

"Leave," he had written beneath it, "come to me." Four words, reaching across an ocean. She never replied.

There are many ways to keep out boundlessness. The man I loved was trapped inside a life as well—I called to him too, asked him to cross over. In the end he also made his choice in that dual economy of love: not to be the lover who spends it all, knowing that passion replenishes only with the giving, but to remain the husband, parsimonious and careful, the one who saves love, who *husbands* it, since he doesn't know how much is in the coffers and so fears squandering it.

What is worth holding onto? What, in the end, are we forced to let go? What simply fades with the holding, leaving us looking down into our own two empty hands?

. . .

These last days in Temecula are tranquil and maddening. The heat has set in, and the cabin becomes a convection oven, the searing winds driving up the valley like a sirocco. By 10 A.M. the sky is wavering like cooking oil above sand the color of bones. By noon the sun pounds down like a fist. By sunset the whole earth is panting, stalled, stunned by this brass-knuckle heat.

I droop over my writing, palm these reluctant pages. For four months I have been trying to tell this tale. I have made it a comedy, a tragedy, an instructional piece, a jumble of aphorisms, a *palatum cordis*—like the medieval monks who needed to taste the word of God with the heart's palate.

I have tried to decipher this eight-year intaglio of a love through paradox. In my mind it becomes the Ship of Theseus, whose planks were all replaced over the years: *If you repair something enough times, is it still what it once was?* Or the paradox of Zeno's arrow: *If there is no movement in instants, one is never able to begin, let alone reach any goal.* I've learned how often truth can be a riddle, like Eubulides' quandary: "Does the man who says 'I am lying' lie?"

Nihil sunt nulla proprietates. In the Megarian theory of eristics, correct inference is impossible. The best we can hope for is avoidance of error. For forty years I have been trying to write this story. Like home, I keep moving towards it and away; it remains a mosaic of fragments that will never fit.

. . .

WHEN WE FINALLY ENDED THINGS, MY LOVE AND I, IT WAS A QUIET step—more a defeat than a rending. It's how things die: they suddenly slip across a threshold from one state to the next. I came back to Ann Arbor, pulled into my drive, shook the recalcitrant wisteria, stepped onto the hardwood floor, and felt my life resume. Losing love means letting go of faith, means moving on. *All things are impermanent,* Buddha says.

On Christmas Day in Mesa I am lying next to the resort's heated pool, looking up at fiery bougainvillea. Beside me, my father is half dozing in a deck chair. The morning is crisp, but already the sky is bright, enameled by the desert sun; and through the vapor of silky, warm waves I see golf carts transporting the elderly to holiday crafts classes, lectures on The Vanishing Rainforest of Brazil. Time is untethered here; death, too, is a featureless resort, well governed but barren.

I look out over the desert, the emptiness that edges all our vanities. What do we have to shore against it? What can be saved?

Last winter my father fell on a tennis court and cracked two ribs. He thought he was mending, but two weeks later a blood clot traveled to his brain and he had to be rushed to surgery. They opened up his head and poked around inside—seventy-four years of stuff in there. The color of his mother's hair. The smell of simmering onions. Schiller's plays. How to use a wrench. Burning his shirt with an iron the morning I was born.

But what he said when he came to was that he'd had a sort of morphine dream, like a movie reel unspooling—a vivid recalling, a re-*feeling* of all the pain he'd ever suffered as a boy, as a man. He lived again the war, his wounds, his operations, accidents, each bodily suffering, every trauma. He thought he'd died, and that this excruciating film was hell.

I look at him now, tanned, sitting in the sun backed by palm trees. I touch his thin old shoulders, lean my cheek to his.

"Dad, what would you take from a burning house?"

He pats my wrists, looks at the sand, and laughs. In all those years it never occurred to us to ask. Feeling his frail, loved body beneath my hands, hearing his laughter, suddenly the riddle opens and I know. I know, for all our wanderings, for all our restless, insatiable desires, we live in a place where night falls fast.

I know, before he says it, the only thing worth taking is the fire.

Preservation: A Story

METHOD 1: AERIAL PHOTOGRAPHY

WHEN WE MAKE LAND, THE JAPANESE BEGIN TO RUN. AS SOON AS THE ferry plank comes down against the small, abraded dock, they gather their luggage and rush past the postcard-pretty cabana toward the white sand and palms. "They always *do* that," the resort hostess chirps, guiding us off the boat. "They have such *energy!*" Like ending a tour of duty, a gaggle of new passengers—burnt dark and tired looking—wait to board.

The ferry ride from Queensland was two hours in high seas. *Twenty-foot swells*, the captain said. His voice was nervous. The Portuguese couple had been vomiting since Cairns. The crew decided to postpone the on-board snack, so instead we watched videos on "The Wonders of the Deep" and "Islands of the Great Barrier Reef" —images of pixilated sun and an ocean blue as mouthwash—while outside a horizon the color of a battleship rose and fell.

"Are you going to lose it?" I asked my sister, who was gazing out a convex porthole crusted with spray.

"In what sense do you mean?" Her smile was frosty, casual.

At that moment one of the scientists on board took the microphone and announced that our destination, Heron Island, wasn't near the reef, it *was* the reef. *Just think, tonight you'll be sleeping on the back of the largest living organism in the world.*

"I thought he meant my husband," a woman muttered.

"It's just me now," my sister had said at the airport, her voice wooden. I wanted to reach for her, but she had already turned away.

Method 2: Drying and Pressing
Method 3: Suspension in Fluid

When we planned this trip, I'd been home doing laundry. She was on the phone from Ohio, long distance in the middle of the day.

"*Colors* in cold," she intoned. "*Whites* in hot."

I told her to save her dime.

"And what if you shrink his clothes?"

Well then, I told her, I would just have to find a smaller man.

I heard the click of call waiting on her end. She buzzed me into dead space, somewhere between Ann Arbor and Youngstown.

How could I tell her that the man I loved *was* shrinking? That his love was growing more distant, like something receding on a horizon? That he was becoming, like me, a better liar every day?

She had her own secrets. Last week she said that she had decided to sell the house. *It's too big now*, she sighed, *and the view was a lot nicer back when we were building it.*

For a long moment I imagined us both on hold, suspended between different lines.

"My lawyer," she announced when she came back on. "I have to go."

Method 4: Freezing Assets

My sister tends to assemble, to hold onto things.

I have a snapshot of us as children, in a field of flowers. She has gathered a bouquet of fireweed and goldenrod as composed and perfect as herself. She looks into the camera coolly, posing with her blossoms, a six-year-old beauty. Beside her, I am clutching one broken parasol of Queen Anne's lace, four years old and staring, absorbed, into its bloody eye.

She was always the collector: eggs, rocks, butterfly wings, feathers. She was lethal and precise—bird's nests, snake skins, the whorled cones of empty hornets' nests like gray paper piñatas. She'd pin and label them, store them in immaculate, logical groupings.

In her twenties she took up photography. The faces of her friends hung frozen, dripping over the darkroom basins. Captured by a cold, flat lens. A guillotine shutter. *My subjects,* she'd laugh, spreading her open hands toward them like a queen.

METHODS 5 AND 6: DESERT BURIAL AND MUMMIFICATION

WE'RE HERE NOW, HALFWAY AROUND THE WORLD, BREATHING THE SILKY, tropical air. The brochures had almost been accurate, everything but the clouds stacking up in huge cumulus piles on the horizon. We follow the crowd to the dining pavilion and gift shop, then we're shown to our duplex condo and semi-private beach. In the suite above us are *two very nice gentlemen,* the hostess states. Later I see one of them on the balcony, seventy if he's a day.

Our suite is cool and beautiful, salt-colored stucco and tropical architecture: tile floors, wood-slatted windows, a patio that leads down to the sea. Even with my sister's settlement, we can only afford four days at this resort—*but it's worth it,* the travel agent had said, *three-star food and a research station on the island.* We unload our snorkel gear, our one or two dinner dresses. At forty-six, my sister still insists on getting to choose which bed is hers.

After sunset I wander down the short path to our tiny beach. The wind is fresh, but it smells strange, swollen. In the dark, the sea is a luminous chemical, the reef a line of white chop where the world falls away.

METHOD 7: ORAL RECORD

I can't believe Mom is making me take you along. I AM FOURTEEN, WEARING fishnet stockings that feel like the web on a rind of cantaloupe, an apricot-colored miniskirt, and white platform shoes. It's 1972, a high-school dance. We're in somebody's father's Lincoln. A canopy of trees silvered by the sweep of headlights.

Up front, my sister pushes the buttons on the radio. *For Christ's sake just don't embarrass me.* The vinyl of the back seat is sticking to my legs through the stockings' tiny crosshatches. When I peel them off later, my thighs will look like they've been grilled.

My sister prods until a Jimi Hendrix song comes on. It's our favorite. *Well she's walking through the clouds, with her circus mind spinning round . . .* I can see her frosted lipstick gleam like something out of science fiction in the greeny dashboard light. *Butterflies and zebras and moonbeams.* She flicks down the visor, looks at herself in the dollar-sized mirror. Her eyes catch mine. For an instant, we are almost in sync.

What should I tell her? That the man I love goes hot and cold because he doesn't know what he wants? Or that it's me who keeps changing from woman to girl and back again at all the wrong times. How can I tell her that the view is always better before the walls go up?

Take anything, anything you want from me, Hendrix sings. But her look snaps shut like a compact; she flips the visor up and drapes her arm easily, possessively, femininely against the driver's dark-profiled shoulder.

METHOD 8: CRYOGENICS
METHOD 9: RUMOR

AT DINNER, THE GUESTS IN THE SUITE ABOVE—WINERY OWNERS, A WID-owed greybeard father and his unmarried son—invite us to their table to regale us with stories of Cawarra and the Murchison Valley. You can almost smell their loneliness. We learn from them that two days before we arrived, a woman had been helicoptered out for shark bite. Swimming at first light, she'd felt a tug—no pain, just a hit like a bolt of current, then a red wash spreading behind her like a wide flamenco skirt. *It happens that way sometimes, so fast you don't feel it till you see the blood.*

The staff had murmured about it for a day, then fell silent and smiled—the official line: to say nothing.

We excuse ourselves soon after coffee. The men rise as we get up to leave the table. "There's going to be a typhoon," the young one says. "I hope you girls came ready for our rains."

He's right. The next day is dusky, the palms despondent, drooping and still in the heavy air before the storm. My sister and I walk along the shore after a late breakfast. Near the marine research station, a cluster of scientists have gathered, excited, taking notes. A nest of sea turtles are hatching before their time, mistaking weather for nightfall. We stand with the scientists and watch the tiny turtles pour across the sand, scrabbling toward the sea. We see the sharks approach, huge indigo shadows trolling the shoreline, and above, muttonbirds and gulls, shrieking banqueters. The hatchlings advance down the beach like green toy soldiers, marching to their demise.

Method 10: Climate Control

"When did you start taking those?"

"Oh, you know. It's just cosmetic psychopharmacology."

She closes the medicine cabinet, smiles. "Come on, let's go be joiners." The staff has arranged a hike around the island in the late afternoon. The paths are sand, peppered with tar and guano. It sticks to the soles of the Japanese tourists' sandals until the bottoms of their feet look breaded.

Our guide explains the island's fauna—points out the nests of muttonbirds that look like molehills rising from the ground. *The adults are excellent fliers*, she says; *they can spend whole days at sea. But adolescent muttonbirds are clumsy. They don't know how to land yet, so they plow into whatever's handy—tree trunks, the sides of dunes.*

"That's us," my sister elbows me.

I once had one fly right into my chest, the guide laughs. *It was like a forward pass with feathers.*

The Japanese laugh too, although they haven't understood a word. They think somehow that she is talking about sheep. A woman from Orinda, California, falls behind. She has only brought high heels, so with each step she sinks deeper into the unstable ground.

The guide describes the tidal currents that part around the island and slowly drag its coral sands into a moving point. An island the shape of a teardrop, trickling westward several inches every year. *I'll bet you can't feel the ground shifting under you, but it is.* That's us too, I think.

We stop to watch a white heron, the island's namesake, standing motionless in a small lagoon. A pale question mark, etched against the gloom of cypress trees and water, its slim beak a dagger, hungry to spear its own reflection from the deep.

METHODS 11, 12: PROBATE, PINNING UNDER GLASS

MY SISTER CLAIMS SHE DOESN'T REMEMBER OUR SUMMER IN MAINE *where in rock pools anemone pulsed, poisonous and beautiful, the starfish in the shallows as fat as bankers' fingers.* There was a swing in front of the ramshackle, six-bedroom farmhouse, hanging from a century-old pine on ropes that could have been twenty, thirty feet long. That swing's arc was big as half a Ferris wheel. *Near the dock, my sister collected blue-black mussels, their mosslike beards tenacious, alive. The soft inner lips were the color of sunset—orange, beige, cream.* I remember pushing off, straining back, then up, back, the lever of my body working its small physics, back and up *and there were lobsters in the large kitchen, my sister holding one half in, half out of the scalding water with scientific calm to hear its needle-like scream* nearly perpendicular, my face to the blue sky, the pine boughs upside-down in air—until I felt the sickening slack of rope as all laws fell away.

METHOD 13: SALTING AND BRINING

THERE IS SAPPHIRE CORAL HERE, AND STARFISH ALL THE COLORS OF CONtusion; strawberry wrasses, sergeant fish, rays. There are brain corals and magenta fans, sea cucumbers stuck to the ocean floor like footlong leeches. We have decided not to snorkel yet; we're waiting to see what the weather does. We are adepts at not venturing into things. The wind chaps the water's surface. The currents below are cold and strong.

We watch the tourists walk the reef at late morning's low tide with tall staffs and strange tubular contraptions made to clarify the depths. They stagger like drunks, knee-deep in water, or reel like daytrippers in a Coney Island fun house, buffeted by gusts. The sky has turned purple. The wind rips a straw sampan hat off a woman's head, and it disappears into the distance, blown over the ocean's close nap, spinning like a Frisbee, like an alien spacecraft out toward Indonesia.

The resort guests wade back toward shore, pummeled and cringing. Palms begin to show the silver undersides of their fronds in the growing gale.

METHOD 14: CATALOGUING

The path was a spine of rock between beach and meadow. My sister recited the names of trees to pass the time. Black ash. American elm. Sugar maple. Sassafras. Tulip tree. *Far below us, I could see jellyfish luminous in the green water, the Atlantic licking grey lumps of rock.* Are you afraid, *she asked. Her eye was the osprey's scream.*

METHOD 15: TANNING AND CURING
METHOD 16: AGING IN CASKS

ALL THAT AFTERNOON WE SIT BY THE POOL, WRAPPED IN TOWELS. WE sip the mango daiquiris the cabana boys keep bringing on their shiny trays.

My sister, bored, has begun reading shark facts to me from her

Swaine's Australia Tours brochure. *You can kill them by dragging them backwards through the water so they drown in their own element. That takes sixteen hours.* She shifts her legs; they are long and rare, the color of candle wax. *Or you can knife them, but you have to hit dead on. They have these bullet-sized hearts, it says, and brains the shape of tuning forks. They're almost impossible to kill.*

Years ago, she had wanted an even tan for her wedding. She'd said it was because tradition dictated that she couldn't wear white again— second marriages were ivory or pastel—but she figured the darker her skin, the whiter that dim, second-time-around gown would seem. I thought it was strange, darkening yourself to appear more virginal.

Listen to this: A man in Tampa Bay, six hours later, patted his stiffening trophy and lost an arm.

I look at her careful, kept body. Her hair has begun to gray.

"Are you afraid?" I ask her.

The sky is the color of gunmetal. Her eyes close behind her Fendi sunglasses.

METHOD 17: DAGUERREOTYPE
METHOD 18: IMPRINTS IN CEMENT

"You're making it up," she says. But I remember the dock we ran down had old wet wood the color of oil. My sister laughing, chasing me with a frond of seaweed. I was barefoot and so began to slide halfway to the water, surfing the slippery planks for one impossible moment—my arms spread, my heart stalling like a surprised engine. Fall, my sister shouted, but I didn't understand. Then I was off the edge and under water, dropping through a green world, murky with rising bubbles.

I sank, stunned, past pylons furry with algae, past the point where gold-brown shafts of light dissolved into darkness. A trance of disbelief and fear. Suspended.

Only after a long while did I begin to kick, rising slowly back up to the water's skin that undulated above me like a membrane of light. My legs churned the darkness, clabbering the ocean into tar, into gold. When I broke the surface my sister was gone. All I saw was the dock's slick edge at least a yard beyond my grasp, and a slice of bright, indifferent sky.

METHOD 19: CHEMICALS

ABOVE US THE STORM MOANS. DOWN HERE IT IS SILENT. IT'S OUR THIRD day and we have decided to go in. This morning I rented wetsuit tops from the island scuba store; below the insulated vests, our legs are so pale they look like streams of milk.

The sea is a heavy, incandescent space. The stuff of dreams. Above us, the pitch of waves pushes upward into a fluid sky. Tiny frills of surf break over themselves in this inverted world and curl into silver crescents just under the surface. Below, the reef unfolds in knobs of coral, and angelfish blade through the water, agitated, tasting the storm's deep source in pockets where the sand boils.

Turbulence above, but down here all is slow-motion: coils, ropes of movement, sand swirling, the invisible current tugging at us like soft teeth. The ocean combs our hair into silky haloes. I look at my sister through the distance of glass and water. Her limbs float, her motions unscroll in luxurious slowness. Voluptuous swoon. Like swimming at dawn. Like a slow circling; then the bloom, the crush of the ocean's love.

METHOD 20: TAR PITS

I DOZE AND DREAM THAT WE ARE LURCHING TOWARD PARADISE AGAIN— the boat rising to its dizzying apex, then hurtling down into the sea's green folds. We go up again, everything lifting, drinks becoming airborne, into that space where gravity falls away, where all natural law is suspended. I can see the steward's tie levitate from its shirtfront, the marine biologist's glasses float for a dreamy moment off the bridge of his nose, my sister's hair undulate above her shoulders like fantastic smoke. Then we plunge down another trough of gray-green water, where time and weight resume.

When I wake, there are nothing but night noises coming through the darkened windows. Tropical notes. Death is out there; but here on land, only the sounds of love, the tinkling of music from the resort cabana, a throbbing shortwave radio from the biological research station, where the scientists sit around with their last half-bottle of Jack Daniels. Upstairs, the vintners dream of the women who might have loved them, who might have peopled their lonely, barren acres. At dinner, a willowy blonde at our table lifted her shirt to show us the dark marks the deep sea currents had left on her ribs and abdomen. *In Belize once I stayed down so long I even had bruises on my insteps.* Poseidon and Tyro, their rough lovemaking.

I rub sleep from my eyes, reach for my credit card. I dial the long number just to hear him, even though it's no more than dawn in Michigan. All I get is the machine—my own voice telling me that no one's home.

The wind bangs like a tin sheet in a school play. Later, my sister comes back alone from the bar. Her eyes look tired, raw, learning to stare into smoky air again. I watch her undress in silence, ease herself into the narrow bed. How can she not know that the sea behind our lives is blooming rubies?

Beyond the surf, the sharks cruise moonlit blue boulevards. The ocean opens inward, a heavy door. The reef is a casement—over its abraded lip is the abyss.

METHODS 21 AND 22: EVISCERATION AND FOSSILIZATION

I think you should be careful of distorting things. You've always been inventive. It's our last morning, and my sister has taken a towel down to the cold beach. Defying the gray sky. She arranges her body with precision, her hair fanned, her chin tilted perfectly at a nonexistent sun.

I put on my snorkel and mask. My wetsuit is still damp, heavy as a tire, and my fins roil up sand, but the moment I plunge in, the world turns clear and light. I feel the sea's hands grip my waist, the outgoing tide hold me in its motion. I let it propel me, dodging the occasional rocks and branches of coral where zebra fish dart and hide.

Below me, the reef glides past with its detritus—fossils, fish bones, shells, all the unclaimed siftings and particles of time.

I just want the current to wash me clean. I don't know what's ahead of me or behind. My heart feels bruised, buffeted by the drag of the past, and the force of what's to come appears tidal and huge, dictated by its own unknowable rules.

I drift, letting the ocean take me, my eyes closing, opening, closing as slowly as mollusks. Gradually, the sea pulls me closer to its edge. I know I am hovering over the lip of the reef when I feel the water turn cold, like a skein of icy fabric. I open my eyes and look down.

All at once, I am dazzled. A school of jacks, gift from the sea, has materialized all around me like a sprung slot machine, an avalanche of silver. For several long heartbeats I am caught up in their wild shine, their perfect dance, as they dart around me in unison, glimmer on all sides like spilled mercury. Unearthly phosphorescence; sudden, sheer harmony.

Then the school parts and I see the sharks. Three of them, eight feet long, thrashing as if to shake themselves free of their own skins, mantled in a backdrop of dark blue where the reef plummets into open ocean. I realize that they have been herding these fish into the wall of rock and coral; now they are about to feed. One approaches me, swerves, then advances again—ten feet away, seven, six, then passes so close I could touch its emery-board skin, could cup the black, inhuman eye that rolls back at me like a savage new moon. My heart lifts in my chest, enters a strange, bottomless space, a swoon of fear. All laws fall away.

I don't know at what point my body begins to lever itself toward shore. I fight the current, the ocean's shoving hands. The journey is interminable, but I cannot look back. Terror paints those giant shadows behind me in the water.

Finally, twenty feet from the shoreline, I stand and look up the beach. My sister is there, waving, as if she is drowning in air. Behind her, the palms sway in a kind of gentle mockery. It occurs to me that she's seen nothing, is merely waving to wave.

I want so much to reach her, but my legs are rubbery, as in a nightmare. Knuckles of coral keep tripping me; my fins drag. She comes down to the water's edge and stands waiting, her arms akimbo, her eyes blank as nickels.

I almost died out there, but the wind steals my voice.

"Are you ready for lunch?" she replies.

———

Epithalamion

When we dream and when we couple, we embrace phantoms.

—Octavio Paz

1. Wintering on the Hudson

At the entrance to the Poets' Walk Romantic Landscape Park of Dutchess County, there is a warning not to walk alone. On the rough cedar pergola, the police have posted their composite sketch of a rapist who attacked a girl here last June. Nearby, Washington Irving has horns drawn on his head, and graffiti offers Keith Haring-like petroglyphs, generic and clumsy enough to be almost endearing, of human breasts and cocks. Anatomy rounded off like a loose equation. *Be smart,* the flier lectures. *Walk with a buddy.*

I take the path anyway, follow a looping necklace of dog prints in the snow. The landscape dips, then rises to a ridge barely distinguishable from the pale, wide waistline of winter sky. To my right, Rokeby Mansion's orchards stand shriveled in the thin light. Further on, the Bard College gymnasium looms like a grey bunker. I imagine white, fat bodies swimming a slow backstroke in the steamy, chlorinated atmosphere; the clang of weights; the sterile whirr of exercise machines. Shelley in the Bay of Larici. A girl shoved into bracken, palm over her mouth. Near here, on the sand plains south of Albany, Vladimir Nabokov discovered a new species of butterfly, *Lycaeides melissa samuelis,* commonly named the Karner Blue after a railway station on the line between Albany and Schenectady. "People go there on Sundays to picnic," Nabokov wrote, "shedding papers and beer cans. Among this, the butterfly."[9]

Below me, the frozen Hudson—turgid, gunmetal-grey sluggard—creeps three hundred miles from Lake Tear of the Clouds to spend itself against the concrete flanks of Manhattan. It has been called the River of the Steep Hills, the Grand River, Rio de Gomez, Rio de Guamas, Rio San Antonio, the River of Prince Mauritius, the Nassau River, the Manhattan River, and the North River. The Mahicans called it *Muhheakunnuk,* "great water ever moving." Stalled now with ice, maculate with slabs of slate colored freeze, beneath its snow-curdled surface iron-grey currents define the river's bones. Below even that, the toxic sludge of a century of industry waits for spring to churn it back into meltwater and motion.

I don't really care about the river; it's just here, like a cellmate I'm going to have to get to know. It is, as one guidebook claims, "trout stream and estuary, water supply and sewer, ship channel and shad river, playground and chamber pot."[10]

It has a long resumé, from which I can sometimes dredge a few interesting facts.

In Columbia County in 1882, a man was apprehended grilling the liver of one of his neighbors, a gentleman he had murdered for a gold button on his vest.

Franklin Delano Roosevelt is buried on these shores, as are Teilhard de Chardin and Dr. Timothy Leary.

Dolphins have been seen swimming as far north as Albany. When they enter sweet water, their skins blister and ulcerate, and they die.

It spawned a school of painters and a style of residential architecture singular in its ugliness.

There are more striped bass in it than there are people in the state of New York.

I've come to this place to write, to think, to *winter*—as that verb suggests something survived, endured, come through. I am going to be married in June—for the first time, at midlife. In these last days of December, at the pivot of the new year, I've found a sudden need to step back and absorb this change. I have my doubts, of course.

What might be seen as an adventure at twenty always seems more like a tempestuous and foolhardy voyage at forty-four. Is it dread or awe that sometimes makes my insides quiver, like an odometer's digits about to fall into a bracelet of zeros? Or is it simply the spirit of Ambrose Bierce's denotative quip: "Bride: *n.* A woman with a fine prospect of happiness behind her."[11]

I've rented a cabin in Ulster County, in the folds of the Catskills, a one-room hut without plumbing, mailbox, phone. By day I read and ski. At night, the blue glow of my laptop keeps me company.

These are the last moments of the year, the century.

All of it—the river's flow, these facts, my meditations—is held in some force's tense, suspended grip.

. . .

A RIVER IS MEASURED IN REACHES, EACH THE DISTANCE THAT COULD BE seen by a skipper in fair weather, point to point. The Hudson is divided into fourteen, among them Chip Rock Reach along the Palisades, Tappan Zee and Haverstraw Bay, Verdrietege Hook, Pyngyp Knob, Seylmaker's Reach, Crum Elbow, Martyr's Reach. Each one has its own character—its own legends, dangers, and tediums. They are like spans of life, fixed markers made up of movement, milestones of transience.

It is strange to be contemplating marriage at forty-four. I feel becalmed by my idiosyncrasies, anchored to my freedoms. I find myself tallying injustices, quibbling about compromise. I can barely recall the flexible, limitless feel of younger love.

Now multiply that integer by two. At fifty-three, my lover is a snarl of habits and routines. We are the King and Queen of Quirk. Sometimes I catch him looking at me baffled, disrupted. He also feels the strain of two old hearts—like hardwood joints—creaking, sometimes painfully, to fit.

When he asked me to marry him, we were standing outside a restaurant in Philadelphia's Little Italy. A warm summer evening, a great *saltimbocca*, and a fair Pinot Grigio; we kissed, leaning on a parked car, while the old Sicilian men on lawn chairs on the sidewalk clapped, and an ambulance squeezed through going no place in particular. He said, *Why don't we make this forever?* And I said, *Why not?* It took us five more months to get a ring.

Sometimes my heart feels weak as putty; sometimes it's arthritic as an old prizefighter's fist.

Since August we have nearly called it off three times. We have lost acquaintances, strained the good will of friends, learned the boundlessness of our bad judgment.

Sometimes my heart shatters; some days it's made of stone.

A friend of mine—a wag—says, "Look at it this way. Soon you'll have the settlement to look forward to."

If you stand very still in the forest, you can listen to nothing but the fine click of wind in the crowns of the empty ash.

. . .

I DRINK BEER HERE, WHICH I NEVER DO—A DARK LOCAL STOUT THAT tastes like tobacco and caramel and wood. I seldom brush my teeth, because I have to lug water up from gas station restrooms in gallon containers, and it's hardly worth the work. My counters are a mess— *my* mess. The wonderful, fertile disorder of solitude. I sit neck-deep in a vast old sofa and read by the hour, eat *biscotti* and shavings off a huge wheel of Brie for dinner.

I love this cabin—its double Dutch door, pine walls the color of honey, a black cast-iron wood stove made in Waterford, Ireland: noisy, glowing, and companionable. The cabin's windows are filled with the shapes of pines, green planes angled against the dimming winter sky. By 4:30 P.M. the light has turned mosaic blue, another winter night falling, the flat light growing luminous, then indigo, then dark in a mantling blackness that still surprises me.

All evening the cabin creaks and pops like an old person's bones—the heat expanding wood, the clack of branches against the roof, muffled rustlings from the forest all around. There's the occasional rumble of a car passing on a distant road, headlights flickering through a quarter mile of trees.

Inside, I have a funky radio, one speaker shot, the other wavery enough to make every announcer sound like Guy Lombardo. I open another beer, listen to "The Thistle and Shamrock," to Tibetan temple chants, to Haydn, to Bob Dylan Live. The stove rips through the cold with teeth of fire.

Later, up in the cabin's loft, the night turns light and dense in alternating waves, as in a dance. Cold, fresh air; warm blanket piles; deep sleep; many wakings, sweet and dream-crazy. A skylight opens up to stars the size of softballs, and Jupiter glowing like a pearl above an oystershell moon. *Mine*, I can't help whispering, giddy as a child. *All mine.*

. . .

MY LOVER HAS NO SENSE OF SMELL, AND HE NEVER DREAMS. HE IS A man of lists and schedules, compelled by repetition. It startles me sometimes how shallowly he lives in this life—all cortex, rule, and plan.

My father was a bit like that. He had trouble with the difference between ritual and routine. He, too, was a little uneasy with the depths.

For me, his life was summed up in a used old tackle box that had been given to him once, an object he venerated like the Holy Grail. My father was no fisherman, but—or perhaps because of it— he'd open that box with reverence, finger each unfamiliar lure as an amulet of mystery and power. He checked out books on fishing, studied the configurations of currents, page after page of crosscut drawings of river bottoms. To him, there was no such thing as luck. Just formula—correct or incorrect—and rule.

I would go with him to the shores of our local lake when the season started, watch him unspool the line, select and attach the lure, position himself, and cast, going through each step in his mind first to get it exactly right.

Needless to say, he never caught a thing—not that summer, not all year. The only things his study earned him were empty afternoons and, at suppertime, my mother's mild derision. I was the only one who stayed with him, staring into the wide green water like Isolde.

Most of the Hudson is rich in fish. It is a murky, protein-dense river, a soup of life stirred by unpredictable tides and currents. Shad grow huge here; bass, pike, pickerel, sunfish, yellow perch abound, though less so these days with pollutants from the paper mills. During the last century, so many sturgeon were caught in these waters that the fish was nicknamed "Albany beef."

Along the wilder upper reaches of the river, brook trout, rainbow, and brown are caught best in late spring with mayfly ties. The names of the dry flies are beautiful: the Quill Gordon, the Hendrickson, the American March Brown, Green Drake, Cahills. The scientific name for the mayfly is *Ephemeroptera*, creature of a day.

You see, I study things like my father did, but impulsively. I cast only for the lucky strikes.

I learn that north of these reaches, up near the headwaters at Feldspar Brook, the waters of the Hudson become so clear you can see thirty feet to the bottom, as if through aquarium glass. The reason for this is that there are no nutrients, and the river is so acidic at its source that no fish can live. Fluke of nature, it is a luminous, lifeless stretch.

Like routine or repetition, it is clear, but empty.

· · ·

I THINK IT MAY BE GIVEN TO SOME WOMEN TO LOVE DIFFICULT MEN. AN industry has grown up around this fact: books on women who love too much, who love too little or too late, who love all wrong. Women who choose badly, deliberately, who *want* to be left or undervalued, beaten, insulted, or destroyed.

It's all crap of course. Women don't fall in love with difficult men. They fall for a man whose smile touches them across a room, a man who makes them laugh, whose walk makes their hearts go soft. It's only later that the complications creep in between them, like sullen stepchildren determined to break them apart, set on reclaiming what was always theirs.

I fell in love with my lover's voice—not only its register, which is a velvety, intoxicating baritone, but the lilt of irony that seemed to be in it, as if he were forever ready to find the humor in things, always on the verge of tipping into a glissando of laughter at the absurd.

One rule I've learned since then is that the complications of complicated men are always the inverse of what made you love them. My lover is, in fact, neither arch nor fun-loving. In real life, he is lachrymose, unmotivated. Despite all his regulation, his finances and relationships are a mess, and he is unable even to tolerate a leaky faucet or a minuscule change in a schedule without leaning his great, sweet head on his folded arms and emitting a series of racking, defeated sighs. I look at him at these moments, and I wonder about many things.

I had a friend once who was difficult in this same way. I had known this man, Roger, in Michigan; but he moved East after graduate school and, not long afterward, met and married a nice, stable woman with a young son. Uncharacteristically for these second-family situations, it turned out Roger and the boy were made for each other. Sam followed Roger everywhere with a molten look of adoration in his eyes. Roger, for his part, had confided to me before the wedding that he loved Eileen and all, but what he really couldn't wait to be was Sam's new dad.

But Roger too had this depressive problem—not depression, exactly, but selective melancholia, like my lover's slightly histrionic, calculated despair. He too would slouch and mope, or slump despondent in the face of household projects or office deadlines. Changes in plan decimated him. Sometimes he would watch the evening news and weep.

One day Eileen burst in on him mooning in their kitchen, and she literally took him by the collar and began shaking him.

"You're going to quit this crap, or you're going to start on Prozac," she shouted. "I caught Sam the other day telling his friends how *depressed* he was. He told Billy Engel how life was sometimes *just too much*. Roger, he's a nine-year-old boy. I'm not going to have him learn how to act suicidal just because he wants to be like you."

Roger went to his doctor and was started on a mild course of Zoloft. He was ecstatic, as complicated men are sometimes when the solution to a problem can be found in a bottle of pills. Eileen seemed sulky but acceptant. At least Roger had stopped the woe-is-me sonata, and Sam seemed to be doing better at school.

Visiting them one weekend, I saw Sam and another boy sitting at the kitchen table, having just massacred a baked-bean and hot dog lunch. Sam was rolling pellets from the soggy paper plates and holding them one by one up in the air.

"Look, Nate," he crowed, "happy pills!"

Then he ate them.

The reason I was visiting that weekend was that my lover had dumped me two weeks before—another, rather major complication, and a habit he seemed to be developing. I hadn't seen Roger in months, not since their wedding, and miserable as I was, I needed some company. Anyway, it was Sam's birthday, so I bought something large and computerized and noisy, wrapped it lavishly, and drove the ten hours to Boston, hoping to bribe my way into the comforting chaos of a prepubescent's party.

There was a friend of Sam's staying overnight as well, a boy from Sam's old school named Nigel, I think—some name that would have been the butt of jokes. He seemed rubber-boned and awkward, always trailing behind the pack of new friends with whom Sam seemed to be having so much fun.

The birthday party was held at a skating rink, a dozen nine- and ten-year-old boys flashing around on high-tech skates, Roger with them, clowning and making Sam feel special. Nigel banana-peeled behind. The moms waited in the bleachers, near an ice-cream cake that said "10!" and a table full of presents. I sat near the moms, but not really with them. My heart felt run over, and what I really wanted was a double bourbon and a good cry, but I tried to concentrate on the colorful parkas that whirled around like a kaleidoscope of normalcy and joy. At one point Roger waved to me, but Eileen intercepted the gesture . . .

"Honey, look out for Nigel!" whom he had almost skated over.

It occurred to me that I was another Nigel, awkward token from the past, trailing behind these moms and boys and Roger in a kind of conspicuous, uncoordinated misery. I was the single female friend from a different city, a different era, slightly suspect because I was the lover of a complicated man, too—and I could see in Eileen's perfunctory glance that there is no sisterhood among women who love difficult men.

. . .

HENDRICK HUDSON, SAILING THE RIVER IN 1609, FOUND THE INDIANS to be peaceful and eager to trade, the women "faire and lascivious." He took several Algonkian braves on board his ship, a forty-last yacht sponsored by Holland's West India Company named the *Half Moon*, and got them purposefully drunk, his officer wrote, "to discover whether they had any trecherie in them." Upriver, things soured. Two Iroquois "sneaked aboard" and were shot when discovered stealing a "Pillow, and two shirts, and two Bandeleeres," and as another tried to come on deck, "our Cooke tooke a Sword, and cut off one of his hands, and he was drowned."[12]

One thing I do know about my lover: he is dishonest in the little things. He salts the truth, evades, misrepresents. It's as if he's stealing back parts of himself from whatever dispersal or oblivion revelation represents to him, as if somehow, because of some past trauma, his true self is forever in need of camouflage. Lying is his version of integrity.

I don't know how I understand this, or even of what importance it is that I do. On a day to day level, his untruths make me crazy, unravel my trust in him hour by hour, lie by lie. Living with a man like that is like trying to place your feet on a floor of water. Even now, I wonder—what is he doing, besides forgetting me? What else will I never know?

Less than a year later, Hudson perished in a small boat on the frozen seas around Baffin Island, set adrift by mutiny, still searching for the fabled passage to "the islands of spicery"[13] that had brought him up past New York Bay. Meanwhile, other white men ventured up the Hudson River, murdering and burning settlements, claiming the land they named New Netherland. Indian resentment grew.

"Their disposition is bad," wrote de Vries in 1643. "They are very revengeful, resembling the Italians."[14]

Maybe my lover's forked tongue is like my strange love affair with solitude, which I was always given to understand was a forbidden thing for women, a Bluebeard's chamber. My mother, I think, longed for it, though it terrified her. She had been taught—by the world, by other women, by the looks of men—that a door shutting behind a girl would be her death. She was crippled by expectation, always too anxious to be accessible, dying to please.

Later, she did her best to forbid her daughters privacy. A rule in our house was No Closed Doors, and if we were silent too long we'd hear my mother's worried step along the downstairs hall, hear her pause by the stairwell, head cocked for sound, then the nervous call . . .

"What are you girls *doing*?"

"*Nuh*-thing," my sister would singsong from her room, but I'd stay silent, stubborn, renegade.

Nights, even as a child, I'd wait until the wedge of light from my parents' bedroom down the hall went out—my father, the man of the house, owned all the lintels and the locks, was master of forbidden space—and I would climb softly out of bed to close my door at last, feeling in the dark the room complete itself, click shut around me, a delicious, uninfringeable dimension.

Our wounds are complex; the walls we take refuge behind grow thicker as we age. He holds himself together with his small deceits; from time to time, I close my doors to stay inviolable.

I owned a scroll once, an antique Chinese rubbing of two drunken holy men reeling down a mountain path, faint with laughter. The gallery owner had explained that these two sots were the divine guardians of marriage and relationship.

"But it's *perfect*," she declared, seeing my puzzlement. "It's about looking askew, seeing double, if you're going to make things work. Love means you sometimes have to see things a little blessedly, forgivingly slant."

. . .

MY LANDLORD AND I SHARE A BEER ON HIS BACK DECK. HE TELLS ME about the cabin's previous tenant, a painter.

"Jee-*zus*, you should've seen the place when he moved out! Paint everywhere—on the walls, on the ceiling—it looked like the Sixteenth Chapel!"

I look at him blankly.

"You know. Michael Angelo."

My landlord is a nice guy, a parole officer in Woodstock. He likes me because I'm clean, and because writers don't use flammable solvents, unless you count Scotch.

He bought the cabin last year from a hunting buddy. The guy had built it after his divorce because his wife lived nearby and wouldn't let him see their daughter. It took her eight months to figure out that he was spending weekends in the woods, trying to catch glimpses of his little girl. She called the cops, had him arrested as a stalker.

We're watching a late blush of sunset over the Ashokan reservoir, which my landlord's house overlooks. I think it is the prettiest body of water I've ever seen—cupped by mountains, dotted with two islands, folded into a perfect curve of wooded shore. I explain to him that *Ashokan* is an Indian term meaning "to cross the creek." Then I list other place names here I've learned: *Kitchawan*, "large and swift current"; *Cohoes*, "canoe falling"; *Taconic*, "full of timber"; *Hoosic*, "place of stones."[15]

"Yeah, that's real interesting," he says, pulling on the seat of his pants. "Did you know Brad Pitt just bought a house up Ohayo Mountain Road?"

That night in the cabin's loft, I gaze up at a skyful of stars. I want to be thinking about the Pequod Indian myth of the goddess who placed the new moon in the sky by first cutting up the old moon and scattering the pieces around the heavens. The bright scraps of stars. I want to be thinking about men who are fathers, men in exile and their complicated loves.

But what I can't help thinking about is Brad Pitt, rain dripping off his Stetson, wearing his blue jeans like an attitude, grinning at Geena Davis through the window of a car.

What gets you about the movies is the vapid certainty of it all—love is right, right now, no doubts, none of this waxing and waning. Obstacles, maybe, but no uncertainties. And afterwards, even if he's disappeared, even if your money's gone, it was real, it was true. Even if it costs you your life, hanging like Wile E. Coyote above a cartoon canyon's vanishing point—hey, it was *love.*

. . .

FUMES, VAPORS OF COLD. A SUDDEN BRIEF SNOW HAS TURNED THE WIND sharp as an edge. The air is crystal-fogged, frozen motes sparkling, spinning in the sun. Everything diamonds.

The ski trail at Mink Hollow curves along a stream, where fingers of pine trail in unguent, tea-gold water. Bracelets of ice hold them down, flashing. Below, trout move the cold slowly through their ivory feathers of flesh, overwintering.

Is it worth it, after all, to keep pulling your heart up from its soil to examine its growth? All this scrutiny, all this effort to leverage a little nerve. Everything here is jewels. Across a clearing I see five deer look up, pausing before flight as if they were remembering another, winged life. Behind them, whitened mountains shoulder the sky, the first smudges of snow clouds trailing over their crests.

All these bits, what do they add up to? Love is the koan of love.

Only my skis keep quarreling with the silence. *Shush, shush. Shush, shush.*

· · ·

I DECIDE TO CALL HIM FROM A VILLAGE PHONE BOOTH TO CHECK IN, SEE how he's doing. I can hear the gladness in his voice. It softens me.

He asks if he can come up so we can spend New Year's Eve together. I remind him that this is a sanctuary.

"I thought sanctuaries always had to take you in."

"Not this kind."

But I *do* want to see him. I've missed his touch, missed waking to his heathery warmth. And New Year's is a holiday for lovers, for ends and starts. We agree he'll take the train up from the city New Year's Eve, then catch a taxi to the cabin. The Rhinecliff station has one cab, the driver a woman in her sixties with a permanent head of curlers. I know she'll get him here.

Afterwards, I drive to the Poets' Walk again to muse on ambivalence. I like this park; it's ratty, circular, with no views to speak of. Appropriate to the perambulations of poets. It's 4:00 P.M., and in the failing blue light the valley is already dark and searingly cold, snow glazed hard as concrete in the sudden wind. Trudging the plotted hills, I think how true that you can only get lost in nature, not in landscape.

What if I took the coward's way, sent up the white flag: *It's not you, it's me.* What if I pulled anchor, called the whole thing off?

The truth: a part of me is afraid of loneliness. Afraid of how much in him I would miss. His tenderness, the sweet crinkle of his chest hair under my palms, the way he closes his eyes in concentration when I read to him.

There is the sense of investment, too: all this expense of spirit can't have been for nothing. This troubled love, this swamp of effort and compromise that has drained us both of so much we held dear. There *are* moments when we see our way clear, when we meet without the need for truce or armament. I confess: I believe in redemption.

I would miss the future, or what I imagine it might hold: travel, trust, maturity. A gradual mellowing into each other, smoothing to a glow like polished wood.

And what of the fear of failure itself?

I was once given a feminist prize called the Susan B. Anthony Award, something to do with volunteerism and *soi-disant* sisterhood. On the plaque was engraved Susan B.'s great dictum, "Failure is Impossible." But the script had strange curlicues, and in the chaos of nerves and klieg lights and applause, I was convinced they had just handed me a plaque that read *"Failure is Impassable."*

I round a bend and see, with sharp loveliness, Mt. Tremper and Platte Clove blazing in the last light, on fire with evening. Twenty miles north of here is Olana, the painter Frederic Church's sanctuary. He waited a decade to buy out the farmer who owned that property, purchase his handful of priceless vistas. "About an hour this side of Albany is the Center of the World," he boasted. "I own it."[16] On it he built his pleasure dome, a thirty-seven-room estate in a style he labeled "personal Persian," where he painted his majestic landscapes: sunsets like red galleons over fairyland precipices and shining water, and—turquoise and ferocious—Niagara Falls, the natural wonder Oscar Wilde called "the American bride's second great disappointment."

Why is pure joy only for the naïve? I think of Percy Bysshe Shelley on the day he drowned, ready to take up the pen again after his swim. Contemplating the great enigma. His desk was as he'd left it, papers ordered, the manuscript of his poem "The Triumph of Life" straightened on the blotter. The last words he had written were *Happy are those who*

. . .

Eighty American rivers are longer than the Hudson.

Local fisherman claim that the nerve endings of the river turtle are so durable, pieces of its flesh will still quiver and squirm on a kitchen counter an hour after it's been chopped up for stew.

The flood tides that run upriver to Rensselaer, and the spring runoff that thunders down from the Adirondack headwaters are two forces so powerful and evenly matched that if you dropped a log into the water at Poughkeepsie, it would take several months to float to Battery Park.

I am stalled, like this river, in a sludge of fact.

I crank up my wood stove, open another beer, read Phillip Lopate: "To travel is to brood."

2. MEN AT FIFTY

JULY, 1978. CALIFORNIA WAS LUSH, ALMOST ROTTEN, THE SUMMER I WENT to work as a weekend writer for the news. I was paying my dues, perched on a cusp between self-importance and lethargy, fresh from college, my mind so open it was empty.

What in hell was I thinking of?

I saw my career sprouting, in a season gone mad as manzanita.

These were the mediaphiles:

Dramatic, overproportioned, fifteen years at the same desk, our Police Reporter was a devotee of disaster. He would "arrive at the scene" to "take a statement," his double knits always more sensational than the crime.

On the Opinion Desk, our resident, out-of-work Keats scholar, taken to six-dollar haircuts and wearing Italian loafers without socks. He called his friends Chancellor and Squire, let great quotes lie about him uncollected, like fallen fruit.

These are the jokes, kid, my columnist friend Stephen said, hiding behind a wall of Scotch, the booze of the news. I had white wine and was nicknamed Prima Donna.

Outside, the summer stank of petrol and magnolia, foot-long franks at the Coliseum, the sweat of athletes and striking supermarket clerks. Bacall made eyes at Bogie across every screen in San Francisco's Tenderloin, days turned odd/even, and somebody won a book award. Then Mount St. Helens blew and Sartre died. Dog days settled in the Middle East, and Morty Miller, old Morty, Uncle M— fifty-six-year-old publican, "slave to fashion," loud, lush, comic mainstay of our Saturday nights—sold his bar for half a million one afternoon and was dead by dinnertime.

What difference did any of it make?

Our public wrote in their opinions: The crossword wasn't printed dark enough. Our comics stank. I switched to Dewars and soda when we drank, read Fran Leibowitz, and laughed when she wrote *I have no ears. I was kidnapped twice.*

These are the jokes.

One day our City Editor walked out of the office and never came back. It's true; he simply disappeared out of his own life: Ken Reed, aged fifty, leaving a second wife and infant son, four-bedroom home and station wagon, career and clubs, and friends who thought they knew him.

Just after noon that day, he stopped at my desk, looking like he was going out to lunch, and handed me a letter. He said I should give it to the boss, but not before 3:00 that afternoon. He assured me with a smile that it wasn't a suicide note—but to be honest, that thought didn't bother me back then. With the naïve honor of the twenty-year-old, I respected people's rights to make choices about their lives, even if it entailed throwing them away, which I suppose in a sense Ken was doing. Self-reincarnation. This part was the mock-death, and afterwards I realized what an important part he had chosen for me to play in it, since death—even the metaphoric kind—had to go smoothly, had to move forward without rescue, for everything else to follow.

I don't even know why he singled me out for his trust, this last cog in a master plan he must have spent months perfecting—while in the newsroom all of us buzzed on, myopic, drunk on ditto fumes and fluorescence and the sham authority of a 110-desk room closed off to the world, where the world invented itself happening.

I waited until 3:00, and I could lie for effect and say it was a slow, solitary vigil—each spastic clock-hand's jerk into the next unit of habitable time taking Ken further away from us—but in truth it was a hectic afternoon, with phones ringing and Mike Eberbach, the on-staff sexual tormentor, hanging around my desk throwing paper clips at the opening of my blouse. By the time I had a chance to look up it was 3:10, and I put the "Back in Five Minutes" sign on my desk and took the letter in to the Editor's office.

. . .

FIFTY IS THE JOINT OF THE COMPASS—THE SELF AS PILGRIM, HERO, wanderer, poised on the brink between departure and return.

In Wallace Stevens's poem "The World as Meditation," written late in his life, Ulysses is constantly coming nearer to his home, his love, the end of his wanderings—but not here, not yet. Like the poem and its own "patient syllables," the self exists in the space composed by desire: circling, homing in, but never complete. There's something to that: always nearing, not yet arriving, the middle of life as the endless approach, the suspended return.

And there *has* been adventure: seduction, shipwreck, bigamy, swinishness, bravery, virtue. Adrift on a raft, hobnobbing with the dead. But at fifty, the prophecy is still unclear, the outcome still murky.

In his fiftieth year, Thomas Merton, the famous Trappist monk, met his Circe and fell in love, the sap rising one more time under the bark of a hermit's solitude. It was the summer of 1966, and Merton broke lifelong vows of solitude and celibacy, falling into a love he wrote about as profound and beautiful and shattering of all his former selves.

Do you wonder what I am thinking at a given moment? Think of the deep and lasting essence of our love: it is the root of all my thoughts. . . . What is my life? My solitude? The determination to be lucid and quiet and to wait, and to nourish the unspeakable hope of deep love which is beyond analysis and so far down it has no voice left. Down there we are one voice: the voice of your womanness blends with the man I am, and we are one being, completing each other . . .[17]

She was a nurse's aide from Kentucky, half his age, already engaged to a boy fighting in Vietnam.

On the level of pure fact: we love each other as we have never loved anyone else, and the love remains. Neither of us will do anything to destroy or falsify it. It will live as long as we live, and we will live forever.[18]

Rumor has it she was sleeping with another young man at the time. She was a girl whom Merton's worldlier friends warned him was "narcissistic" and "immature."

We have really done this and done it much more than lovers ordinarily do. We are really in possession of one another's secrets, the inmost self of the other, in its glory and its abandonment. To have seen this in each other as we have seen it is a great gift of love, a great creative joy, one of the greatest and most awesome gifts of life: let us never forget this. Let us cherish the secrets that we have exchanged, more beautiful than any ring or symbol of union, secrets that are unspeakable and cannot be explained to anyone for we alone will ever know them . . .[19]

Jezebel? Or was she, too, a part of God's mystical, proffered world?

No one can ever prevent us from thinking of each other and from loving each other. No one can change the fact that we belong to each other. That we have been through experiences of an incomparable love upon which no human being is entitled to pass the slightest judgment.

They have taken away love's compass and instruments, except the rare and secret ones in our hearts, of which we can never be deprived.

What will I be without her? What will she be without me? . . . She will always be to me her soft voice speaking out of the depths of my own heart saying that the central reality of all is found in our love that no one can touch and no one can alter.[20]

Denis de Rougemont called love the highest act of the imagination.

His arms would be her necklace / And her belt, the final fortune of their desire.[21] "The fact that you *are:* that you *are you,*" Merton wrote. "This is all I have left. But it is the whole of love. And nothing can change it."[22]

. . .

IN A LIFE FILLED WITH LOVERS, IT WAS PICASSO'S AMOUR OF THE EARLY 1930s—a model named Marie-Thérèse Walter—whom he could not get out of his mind for the rest of his life. He met her the year he turned fifty, and three decades later it was still her face, painted from memory, that twisted in anguish in "The Rape of the Sabines"; hers the remembered bliss, the rapture of peace, in the visage and form of "Sleeping Woman."

Does love at fifty mark a man's soul so deeply it is the oar he carries inland, into death?

When she first sat for him, Picasso was moved to compose something very strange. He fashioned a complicated wire construction which looked like nothing but a meaningless snarl until a light was shone upon it. At that instant, one could see the shadow it projected was the lifelike profile of the woman he so desired, Marie-Thérèse.

Someone is moving / On the horizon and lifting himself up above it. / A form of fire approaches. . . . It was Ulysses and it was not.[23]

What the artist did next is revealing, too.

In a rare moment of self-revision, Picasso changed the construct. First he filled it with plaster, then he sculpted it into a splendid, abstract form. It ended up being a beautiful work of public art, one of his finest.

But the secret image of woman, which for a moment had been illumined, was forever lost.

3. STORM

DECEMBER 31, THE LAST DAY OF THE YEAR, AND THEY ARE PREDICTING snow—a blizzard, a nor'easter. All morning, the radio in my cabin cackles news: six inches expected, then twelve, then seventeen. By noon the actual predictions taper off, and the meteorologists' voices take on a vague, thrilled cast. This is what they've been waiting for all these years, this lifetime of partly cloudy afternoons.

I drive into Woodstock to buy supplies. City women in minks, loath to lose an afternoon's shopping, patrol in pairs down a gauntlet of boutiques. A man in dreadlocks is walking down the center of Rock City Road, bashing his chest with both fists, shouting, *Son of a bitch!* A cop car rolls calmly behind him, the officers sipping coffee out of green and white Starbucks cups. On the town square kiosk, posters announce that Jesus Christ will be speaking on Worker's Rights; that the Animated Trinkets are playing tonight at the Jewel Heart Music Club.

The librarian in the Woodstock Public Library, a guy with a long grey ponytail and a tattoo from Pat's Tats on Route 28, says he wouldn't cross the Kingston–Rhinecliff bridge under snow—*not for a hunnert bucks,* he says, *not for nothing.*

"You into birds?" he asks, holding up the copy of Ted Hughes's *Crow* I'm checking out for snowbound reading.

I look into Pegasus Jewelers, browse the gleaming cases. The owner and I chat about the snow, then about weather reports in general.

"They're always wrong," he chuckles. "I remember the gal who phoned in from Glens Falls one winter, right in the middle of the weather guy's segment. '*Partly cloudy?*' she yelled on the air; 'Mister, I got six inches of partly cloudy on my lawn, and more coming down!'"

He sees the modest diamond on my finger.

"Can I show you anything special?" he asks, drifting toward the wedding sets.

"What've you got in gold chains?"

We both laugh.

The girl in the soap and candle shop next door points to my expedition jacket. She says her boyfriend bought her one just like it for Christmas, but she hasn't tried it on yet.

"It seems so *thin*," she says, making the word two syllables. Her lips above her chin stud are glossed red as a stop sign.

I explain the shell is Gore-Tex; it'll keep her warm outdoors.

"Like, I don't *think* so," she inflects. "I mean, I don't *do* outdoors."

It looks more and more as if outdoors is going to do us. Grey, swollen tides of cloud pour down over Guardian Mountain; restless thermals suck them upward into a white sky, then beat them back like a dark rope-pull of weather. Fronts clash, the snow-heavy clouds making visible the gyrating bodies of moisture and frozen air.

The Grand Union grocery store is crowded, people joking with each other a little nervously about the storm, pulling toddlers and loaded grocery carts out to their suvs. My cart looks strangely skeletal in the checkout line: stout, orange juice, *biscotti,* more Brie. A few more weeks, I think, and it'll be my turn to pound my chest and shout.

Just as I get back to the cabin, the snow begins. A few light flakes on my hair, my eyelids, as I walk the long path through woods to the door. Tiny frozen kisses, the silvery touch of some frosted New Year's angel. A giddy swirl. A wind-tickled flurry.

Then, as I look up into the heavy daylight, the storm begins in earnest, steady and purposeful, as if the sky had torn a seam to dump its stuffing: big cotton balls of flakes. Serious vertical snow.

· · ·

2:30 P.M. STOVE GOING. *Biscotti* CRUMBS EVERYWHERE. THE MICE WILL have a cotillion tonight. Outside, chef's toques of white have accumulated on everything. The birds are silent, the world still as waxworks. Snow pouring down like ticker tape.

The source of a storm, like the source of a river, is never where you think. Even if you could find the very start, how do you define the first drop that begins its course to the sea? Where do you put the clouds that distill into that drop, the wind that moves those clouds, the air mass that stirs the wind? The basis of things is never in one place. The radio says this storm comes from the South. Tomorrow I imagine us shoveling Gullah Island spindrift, Savannah dew.

At 4:00 P.M. I have cabin fever, have to take a walk. It feels like the climax of the storm. I pull on boots, gaiters, Gore-Tex; when I open the cabin door, a knee-high cliff of snow pours over my doorway. I splash into white, along where I remember, vaguely, the path used to be, push through the snow-fogged air toward the ghost of a road, the phantoms of other houses. What lights there are are fuzzy in the frozen haze of blizzard. It is a wonderland—silent, buried, swirling.

A mile down Cooper Pond Road, hot from the trudge, I take off my gloves to cool my hands and look down at the abrupt color my flesh makes in this white-and-grey pixilated world. I see the ring on my finger, the gem's flash on what I suddenly recognize as my own aging hands—faintly freckled, nicked with scars, beginning to wrinkle—hands that look like my mother's did when she was 40 and I thought her so antique, so vestigial to my young life.

Snowflakes land on my skin and melt. This same urgent, relentless snow that erases landscape, fills in roads, buries landmarks, merges the world's detail into this white figment. I put my gloves back on. *Not dead yet,* I think. Ringed round with circumstance, I still steer my body through this world.

By 6:00 I'm home, my clothes drying over a chair. It's dark now, but the snow continues, a paradox of white exfoliating from black. Cheery voices on the radio announce that St. Bridget's Catholic Church in Cornwall Bridge has canceled vespers; Salisbury Liquors, Hoosatonick Fitness, and the Bargain Barn are closed. Confession at St. Jude's in Lakeville has been called off. I open a can of soup, turn the station to soft jazz. The stove chortles, chews on its fuel.

The cabin's heat and the music make me doze. I wake at a quarter to nine, pulled out of a dream of tornadoes and trains. *He's coming*, I think, and my heart jumps; then, *He'll never make it.* The tracks along the Hudson pile up fast; there'll be delays. With a pang, I envision him spending New Year's in Penn Station. Suddenly I want him here so badly, I'm trembling. Is this what love means? This weakness, this sudden, searing need?

．　．　．

IT'S NEW YEAR'S EVE, THE NIGHT OF JANUS, GOD OF DOORWAYS. GOD of beginnings, philoprogenitive, no father or mother. The one Roman deity with no Greek counterpart, no cousin on Olympus. God of two faces—past and future—looking back, looking forward.

In the Roman ceremonies on the Campidoglio they would sacrifice white oxen, first gilding their horns and garlanding them with flowers. The giving up of something precious ensured good fortune for the year. All around, one chronicler wrote, "the air quivering with incense."

I recall a story about French missionaries, baffled by the savage ways of the Indian. One young Jesuit priest wrote in his journal of an Iroquois boy captured by the Huron, led to his torture and death in plumage and ceremony, singing. The whole congregation of his enemies treated him as the honored guest, the hero they would adorn and flay and, by morning, burn alive, whose flesh they would eat and scatter. The priests were horrified by this savagery, nauseated by the brutality of consuming sacrificial flesh. These men with their chalices and scapulars—these men who celebrated the Eucharist every day.

And what of marriage, that sacrifice ordained by bliss? The death of the self into a new life of union. Another ordeal you go into, singing?

So much confusion. Or worse: so many variations on certainty. Proceed. Halt. Love. Leave. Argue. Heal. Play. Fold. Outside, the snow continues—resolute, definite—the sky scattering wild fistfuls of rice.

. . .

IT'S PAST 11:00. THE STORM HASN'T EVEN SOFTENED ITS MUSCLE. THE township plows have given up, their tracks already concealed by drifting mounds as if they'd never been. The only sign of their passing is a wall of plowed snow and gravel that covers half my car.

I'll keep this vigil up until midnight, let the fire die down. The windows yawn black, boiling with windblown snow. The maw of nature, passes piling up with white. In the arc of light from my cabin, I can see the flakes making the wind visible, dressing it in a pallid, swirling sheath so you can see its ligaments, the muscular flow of its dance. Ghostly, the crowns of trees bend in a sudden gust, mesh together and spring apart as if taken by an inexplicable desire.

I've almost given up, am ready to turn out the lights and sleep this century off, when I hear it: the revving engine of a car reversing, a door slammed, the muffled crunch of footsteps in the snow. The fire roars, the windows are jewels in the storm, and my heart flashes and gleams like this firelight on wood. Then he's there, standing in the circle of swift light, and the cabin is no longer a place for one. It is a golden haven, a magnet, a welcome home.

Will you take me across your threshold? he smiles. He has snow frosting his hair, his moustache, even his eyebrows, under which his laughing eyes look out—warm, sea blue, the sweetest look I've ever seen. Reaching for him, I think, *How passion simplifies everything.*

Behind him, the sky is falling.

4. FRAIL VESSELS

THERE IS A NEW GLASS PITCHER ON THE TABLE, THE LIGHT FILLING IT LIKE some precious, pale fluid through which the shortened January day is bent into beauty. Around it, the relics of real life are strewn: a crusty salt and pepper shaker, a jar of buckwheat honey, an empty short-bread tin, a bottle of vitamins, an old phone bill. My lover's break-fast table, and my recent gift to him: this handblown glass which rises, as I would like to rise, above the detritus of his dailiness—sleek, exquisitely fragile, rare and clear.

When I came back to the city, the first thing we did was fight—hugely, shatteringly—about lies and money. For the span of every argument, I think we hate each other. During those moments, hours, we each look with shock into the eyes of a stranger, have trouble imagining how we ever believed we could share a life.

Now we've made it up again. It is a strange miracle, a tenuous resurrection. Sore and wary, we patch together this love one more time. A love of seconds, remaindered pieces.

As the salespeople say, *It gives it character.*

Or is it my mother's voice I hear, steering me from Lalique to Baccarat: *Never buy the flawed ones, honey, they just won't hold up.*

But for the time being, we are mended, although I can still feel our pride beneath the surface like a fault line or a fissure, waiting to spring.

. . .

WE HAVE DAYS OF SOCIAL CHORES AHEAD OF US, THE DRAGGING TAIL OF the holiday season. I need to go up to Princeton to tidy my grand-mother's gravesite, an annual obligation; he has promised to visit an old professor of his who was moved to a new nursing home in that same town six months ago.

On a clear, cold afternoon we make the drive, the sun through the windows and Mahler on the radio making truce between us. He's told this man he would bring me, the "new girl." We've been involved for over half a decade, but time works in strange loops for the eld-erly, and the old man keeps asking petulantly after my lover's first wife, long since divorced.

"'Corporal works of mercy,' my mother used to call this." I gaze out the window with feigned patience.

A lapsed Catholic like me, my lover laughs.

The pretty stone colonials of Mercer County roll past like a Currier and Ives Christmas print.

"Shouldn't we be bringing something? Magazines or chocolates?"

He shakes his head. "He's proud. He'd feel patronized. You know, at the height of his powers he ruled an empire."

"That's a strange image."

"Before he started drinking, he launched a whole generation of scholars, thinkers. They owe him and he knows it, but nobody comes around anymore."

He tells me the story of this man's decline—obsessed late in life with one of his graduate students who spurned him, feeling his slackening grip on fame, then years of liquor, his slow love affair with oblivion, in and out of detox units and emergency rooms, passed out on motel room floors, until he drank himself into a dead end of nursing homes. At first he made the circuit of the elegant ones; in each, he'd settle for a month or two—affluent, gregarious, welcomed for his intelligent Southern charm—until sobriety became too much again, itself another sorrow to drown, and he'd be off, bribing some taxi driver or attendant to help him into a bender. Naturally, the administrators had asked him to leave residence after residence.

"He's been in this new place half a year," my lover says. "I have the name written down. His kids say he's safe there."

I knew the children of alcoholics, knew how frail and tense those relationships can be. A lifetime of resentments, instability, their world drained nightly from the bottom of a glass.

"He's a proud man," my lover repeats.

I envision him shrugging off his children and their remiss obedience, lambasting friends and their inept attendance. I imagine an old knight listing in his armor, lonely and stiff-necked as Lear.

. . .

WITH MERCY—AS WITH DRINK—WE SPEAK OF *tolerance* AND *capacity.*

My mother in her forties, the same age I am now, used to visit the elderly as a work of kindness, fortified and complicated by her own terror of age. She claimed it was her religious duty, but I think she also missed *her* mother, who had died suddenly and too young for care. Perhaps she saw her reflection in the frail and ghostly strangers who were now her special wards. My mother often had a circus of motives for the nobler things she did.

I remember as a teenager being forced along, my reluctance at being dragged through those reeking halls like something out of Dante. "They *like* to see young people," my mother would scold. "It's not a lot you're being asked to do." But it was. She was forcing me to stare into the face of age, and worse, at the visage of mercy—and of the two, I couldn't decide which made me more squeamish.

The Cardinal Nursing Home, the special object of her attentions, was situated on a rise in the town where we lived, overlooking a sweep of small working-class houses, a bend of the muddy river that had named the county, and in the distance the toilet-plunger dome of the Armenian Orthodox Church, flanked by the steel geometry of office buildings and fire stations. The nursing home had an odd vantage in being the highest point in an otherwise topography-free landscape, as if the dying and the lingering were forever looking down at the rest of us, already having begun by a few feet their liftoff into the beyond.

Every Sunday after Mass, my mother would sweep through the Cardinal's wide glass doors and briskly walk the gauntlet of old men parked along the corridor in wheelchairs, who sat looking after her in puzzlement, as if she were some half-discerned, speed-blurred apparition. "Good morning!" my mother would warble; "How *are you* today?" I would slink along behind her in shame, keeping my distance from the chrome chairs and their fixed, unmoored inhabitants.

I was mortified once when one of the men, inscrutable and

antediluvian as a hermit crab, began to weep as I walked past. *"Mom,"* I hissed at her receding form—and what I really meant was *See what you've done.* My mother turned and knelt by him without a pause, gentle and giving. I was horrified, fourteen years old and burning with disdain. *Yes,* she crooned, stroking the man's wrinkled wet cheeks over and over. *Yes, yes.*

.   .   .

WE PULL UP TO A RED BRICK BUILDING IN A NEIGHBORHOOD OF SLUM houses and taco joints, unshoveled snow on the sidewalks trampled to brown sludge. My lover tightens; I can see this is not what he expected. Three or four women in white uniforms are smoking cigarettes and shouting with laughter just outside the doors—inside, the front desk looks like the bulletproof window of a drive-up teller's booth. We wait for a long while before someone comes, a girl whose hair sticks straight up from her scalp so that she looks like she's just woken up from a bad dream. We give the name; she hasn't heard of him. We ask her please to check. *Check what?* she says.

We finally find the room number in a ledger and are buzzed through to the main lobby. The smell is like a slap, a suffocating cocktail of urine and feces and medication. We cross a dim, hairy carpet to the elevator, emerge on the third floor, which the receptionist has warned us is the "zombie zone"—*for the rehabs and the Ronald Reagans,* she smirks. The hallway here is a din, fractured by the noise of rap music from a radio, a clatter of IVs and cafeteria trays. Wheelchairs are parked everywhere, sagging with human-shaped cargo, and the stench is almost unbearable.

Walking past one woman, I hear her keening, reaching up to me with gnarled, useless hands. She smells of pee and plastic, and there is something urgent and painful in the sounds she is making. Six feet away, an attendant behind a desk is laughing with a boy who looks like he's just come in off the street, wearing a headscarf and a whole lot of pants.

What would my mother have done? Made a scene probably, taken the attendant by the forearm, scolded her into attentiveness. It was another era. She was a better woman than I. It occurs to me how much of bad character is made up of the things you cannot bring yourself to do.

"What's taking you so long?" my lover grumbles, and I snap in sudden anger. That argument between us rises from its shallow grave. I turn from the agitated woman, and we walk into the professor's room side by side, bristling like cats.

The room is so dark, it takes a while for our eyes to adjust. Gradually I make out a basin, an empty wheelchair in the corner, somebody's kitschy poster of Jesus on the Mount, a sideburned Christ with eyes like a dachshund's. *Blessed be the Meek.* The walls are the color of prosthetic limbs, and then I notice that the windowsill is lined with books—Proust's *Remembrances,* Himmler's diaries, Huysmans, Martin Buber.

The professor is sitting upright on a bare mattress, a thin blanket tangled around his legs. He is elegant, handsome, completely and tragically sentient. "Welcome, you two. How marvelous to see you." He motions me to the room's single chair as if ushering me into a gracious home.

"Forgive the spare accommodations."

I remark that one chair seems a bit confessional.

"My dear, nothing would please me more than to hear *your* sins." He leans toward me, silver haired, with his honeyed Carolina accent. The old emperor.

My lover and he trade reports of professional politics, masculine gossip, while outside the radio blares and the zombies make indefinable sounds. They begin to speak of this place; the professor describes his roommate, an Alzheimer's patient who spends all night whistling and staring into the basin mirror in the dark, adrift in the lagoon of his own reflection. "It's intolerable, really," he says calmly. "I don't think I've slept one night since arriving here."

My lover engages him with sympathy and sensitivity. He is gregarious and sociable—more to the point, my lover is Irish to the marrow. His is a race that rises to burials and comes alive at wakes. A people that resonate to lament: the sweet, tireless, rhythmical human *ceilidh* of complaint.

My people are efficient, militaristic, practical. Grief needs to be solved like an algorithm, bad feelings sorted out like laundry. We are not brooders or keeners. We are no savorers of sorrow. Our only sentimentality tends towards the operatic, or the plucky wholesomeness of Hummel figurines.

That is why I'm becoming frustrated now, seeing this man in these inhuman circumstances. I decide we have to do something for him. We have to get him out of here. I am already making plans, scheming a rescue operation.

Suddenly the professor begins to speak of his family, and his voice turns gravelly with rage. "My wife was an alcoholic," he barks, glaring at me with unfamiliar eyes. "*That's* why my children are so disturbed." I look at my lover, puzzled. He motions me not to contradict. The emperor goes on spinning. "My son is a recovering drunk, too. Took after my wife. Now he's nothing more than a walking slogan. You tell him, 'Nice day' and he says 'That's your addiction talking.'" The professor picks at his blanket, looking suddenly older, lost, deceived. "Well. You can give your children everything, but you can't make them love you."

There's silence for a moment, then he gazes at my lover with a smile.

"Where's your lovely wife?" he says.

. . .

THERE WAS ONE WOMAN IN PARTICULAR MY MOTHER WENT TO SEE, AN octogenarian named Mrs. Keyes, who always looked a bit alarmed when my mother came in to fling back the curtains and plump the pillows, chattering news of the day. She would lie in bed, frail and slight and ivory-colored as a crumpled piece of old lace, following my mother's movements with her ancient pebble-eyes, and it was impossible to tell just how she felt about the sudden swirl of energy and cheer that was my mother, or the sullen lump of girl she'd brought with her who stood in the shadow of the doorway wishing only to be gone.

Mrs. Keyes had a hobby my mother encouraged: the old woman knitted indistinguishable things with giant knitting needles, the kind made for the sight-impaired or the very young, that formed stitches the size of belt loops. They were so big that it looked as if her tiny, bony hands were struggling with two lengths of plumbing pipe. My mother brought her skeins of wool in wild, Mardi Gras colors—electric blue and eye-searing orange, party pink and fuchsia—and in return was gifted with eight-inch-long scarves and gnarled squares of yarn my mother generously called potholders, but that looked more like the shingled motel roofs of Howard Johnsons.

When my mother got these items home, she would carefully unravel them, then wind the yarn back into balls to bring to the nursing home again next week—the self-designated engineer of Mrs. Keyes's Sisyphean endeavors. Both women were tireless; for months, my mother and Mrs. Keyes labored in their respective parts of town, the one knitting and the other unraveling—the one inventing and the other undoing, like Penelope, the week's creations in some strange and strangely poised dance. *Confounding the Fates,* my father quipped when he passed my mother at our kitchen table, surrounded by the frizz of day-glo orange yarn.

. . .

THE FATES ARE NOT SO EASILY UNDONE. YEARS AGO, MY LOVER AND I spent some time in Venice, and we took a day trip to the island of Murano, where they make the famous glass. We weren't very sure of each other yet, were making those first vague gestures toward revelation; at one point he bought me a trinket—a tiny pyramid in blood-red glass, inutile and beautiful. I held it in my palm all day, feeling its smooth heft like the promise of something solid, something I wanted to be true.

The ferry took us on to Torcello, a strange dream-landscape with its one-eyed campanile and its ancient chapel with the Byzantine Madonna, a girl in a tub of gold with eyes the color of mud—rigid, immobile, and divine. We ate lunch at a restaurant where red hens bobbed like rusty oil drills in the dust around the tables, and German patrons stared at the *calamari* on their forks as if they were being asked to dine on plumbing washers.

It was probably the heat, the wine, the waiter who flustered us by saying, *And for your wife—?* I didn't realize until we were back on the ferry that I'd left the gift behind, on the table beside my napkin. I wept at the bad omen, something given to me so briefly and already gone.

. . .

I NEED TO EXTRICATE MYSELF FROM THIS ROOM RIGHT NOW. THE SMELL of death and self-deceit has thickened in my throat, and I mutter something about errands, my Oma's grave. I stand, and my lover rises too with abrupt tenderness, puts his hand on my coat sleeve, folds my scarf across my neck. "Are you dressed warmly enough?" Full of something unspoken, I cup my palm around his cheek, touch my thumb gently to his lip.

"Don't spend all your money," the emperor croaks from the bed.

And suddenly I realize that that is *exactly* what I want to do: I want to spend it all, this instant, to find something ridiculous that I can't afford and then afford it, exuberantly and without regret. My grandmother's gravesite is fine as it is, a nub of granite under snow. I hear her voice echo a proverb which as a child I never understood: *Lass die Toten die Toten beerdigen.* Let the dead bury the dead.

I promise to be back in an hour. Outside the doors of the nursing home, I turn in the opposite direction from the cemetery and stride through Palmer Square, past an Alhambra of shop windows. Their lintels read Laura Ashley and Restoration Hardware, a landfill

of lingerie and Mission lamps and merino wool. I turn into a sump-
tuous store, all stemware and pottery, and there the one, perfect
pitcher catches my eye, as if it had drawn me to its side. Its body is
a shining sweep, its handle a fluid rope of glass, delicate as a musical
signature. It looks as if it had just this moment been molten into this
precise and tenuous shape, and might, when picked up, pour not
water but itself again into one continuous stream of light.

The saleswoman polishes and wraps it, smiles when I choose a
red ribbon: semaphore of love.

"For someone special?"

"Yes."

"Is it for Valentine's Day?"

I shake my head.

"His birthday?"

"No. It's nothing." But what I mean is, it is everything. Accident.
Miracle. Paradox.

The gift, after anger, of a diaphanous, breakable thing.

. . .

WHEN I GET BACK, MY LOVER IS WAITING FOR ME IN THE LOBBY.

"They said they had to bathe him, so they threw me out. He
wanted to tell you goodbye." He pauses, looking bewildered and gentle. Behind him a wide-screen TV is blabbing at an audience of wheelchairs; a pale, folded-up man parked beside the door has begun to shout.

"Don't ever leave me in a place like this," his voice crumples.
Then he holds my shoulders in his hands. "Don't ever leave me at
all." His grip is as hard as hopelessness, and standing there with my
red-ribboned gift I want to make him all the promises that I know
will have to break and break again and be remade.

We kiss, long and clingingly in the middle of this misery, the
strange aphrodisiac of a roomful of reeking, abandoned souls.

. . .

MRS. KEYES DIED THE SUMMER I TURNED FIFTEEN. I THINK SHE COULD no longer sustain my mother's corporal acts of beneficence. Until the end, my mother would brisk in, flinging curtains open to the sunlight, tidying cabinets, sometimes dusting the dresser with the Kleenex she carried perpetually in her handbag.

Only once in all those months did I get close to Mrs. Keyes. It was a moment when my mother had left the room, and to my horror the old woman motioned me to stand beside her. Reluctantly, I complied. Drawing near, I noticed how small and bald she was, like a flower stalk whose petals had all fallen off in a wind. What was left was nothing but pith and husk, and a dry rattling that was sometimes her breath and sometimes her voice and sometimes, I suspected, the evanescent flatulence of the old.

"I think your mother doesn't like disorder," she whispered. It was the only remark she'd ever addressed to me. Then she smiled and patted my hand. "And you and I know death is a mess."

My mother is now nearly the same age as Mrs. Keyes. Her skin is delicate and wrinkled as the rind of some ethereal fruit; her eyes have become pale as a January sky. Sometimes she looks in the mirror for a long time, dislocated, absent from herself. She looks to me now for kindnesses she barely understands.

. . .

Hand blown in Kilkenny, Ireland, THE LABEL READS. I TRACE THE VESSEL'S shining form, notice the pontil iron's mark dimpling the base like a glass navel, a birthmark, each piece unique. The brochure provides directions for washing, lilts cautions about intemperate heat and cold. *Treated with care,* it croons, *your glass will last a lifetime.*

"But what is that?" I wonder. "What is that?"

5. Banns

I WILL TELL YOU A STORY ABOUT LEAVING THINGS BEHIND. IT TAKES PLACE years ago, when I first met my lover, and it moves its small plot across Italy and France. It ends in an airport in Paris—or maybe it ends here, years later, in a bedroom near an ocean, where I have woken early, before light, to write out my thoughts in the dark while he sleeps beside me.

It begins, at any rate, in an airport: the international terminal in Milan, where I have taken this man I love—eight years younger than he is today, many turns more innocent—to board a plane back to his other life. We have had six extraordinary, unexpected weeks together, and now in this crowded foreign space, stifling with summer heat and the noisy sentiments of strangers, they're ending.

"*We* are ending" is the thought that at that moment wants to insinuate itself, that I want to keep from me but that is already hardening my kiss, fixing my lips into a false, brave smile. No tears. Not even a turn when I walk back through the doors and out into the blazing parking lot, all of Lombardy hot as a kiln. I am at once fatalistic about this terminus and superstitious as Orpheus, hoping he will still be there behind me if I just don't look.

It takes me three tries to leave the hellish traffic circle that keeps bringing me back to the departure gates; finally I am on the highway again, driving through the plains of Brescia which are blurred by unspent tears and heat mirages. I don't quite know where it is I'm going; I have two more months of travel here, a car, a bank account, and an address book filled with the names of past acquaintances I don't particularly want to see.

All I want right now is to get out of this heat. My finger traces the grade-schoolish colors on the map beside me, glides across the brown of northern Italy towards the green and then the silver-grey of mountains to the west of Turin. My index finger taps twice on the wrinkled span of the Alpi Graie. I can almost feel the cooler altitudes through the cheap paper. There. *Andiamo.*

It is my year for flipping coins. The reason I am here in Europe at all is to immerse myself in luck. I have been chance-starved, over-controlled for the last six years. Fast-tracked, promoted, titled, rewarded, emptied out, stuffed and sewn up—at thirty-six I have been taxidermied into the shape of something triumphal and unnatural, the glass-eyed death's grin of a successful, by-the-books career. I needed this year off, my self-styled sabbatical, to relearn the sweet wild truth of serendipity, the force of accident. Others travel to find themselves; I've come to *lose* myself again.

And so I've herded sheep in the South of France, hiked the Pyrenees, stared at the shaggy cattle of Corsica, drifted to Italy, and fallen in love. The last with a man whose complications are immense and daunting, who lives a thousand miles away, is snarled in another life, is as unlike me as chalk from cheese, and for whom I feel I have been waiting forever. You cannot reason with your heart; sometimes you cannot even tell the twins of Chance apart: Fortune from Disaster.

It's two more hours' drive in stifling heat before I see the mountains free themselves from the horizon—dimly, at first, no more than a mirage. Wisps of white above the silvery heat waves, pale trails that could be nothing more than a line of clouds, but that gradually take the sure shape of snow on a serrated blue line of peaks. I want to leave this parching openness behind. Reclose my heart, regain a steady climate, move into the next thing that awaits me.

When I finally come to the foothills, still there is no relief. A traffic jam develops outside of Asti—some summer rock concert, tents wobbling in the public park, a sound crew torturing the amplifiers with barks and shrieks that give voice to this maddening, electrifying heat. Stuck for an hour, I bang my palms against the steering wheel, waiting for the Italians to creep forward in a lava flow of metal and rubber, stall, debate, explode with expletives, then creep forward another meter or two toward the entrance to a hopelessly packed municipal parking lot, where the sole ticket-taker has just gone on a break.

Somebody tries out the sound system again—the wail of an electric guitar string yowls over the city, then an adenoidal roadie's voice mugs the first lines of Dylan's "Tell Me, Momma" in strangely elasticized English. Through the rear windshield of the car ahead of me, I can see two Italian children making faces at each other—fingers in their noses, yanking down their eyes and launching their tongues in the universal ghoulish face-pulling of the under-ten and bored. One looks at me, and on a whim I join them, racking my face into a rubbery devil's mask. Take that. I see them shrieking in soundless delight through the glass.

It's dinnertime by the time I get to Pinerolo, and I spend the night in a small *penzione*, holding onto my heartache like the coin you know will always have the same face on both sides. By morning, the air has changed, freshened. I drink an espresso in the small courtyard before setting off, breathing the scent of chestnut trees and pine. The road gets steeper now; by noon I've crossed the pass of Sestriere, the road sinuous as entrails, the blur of Italian bikers skimming the sides of cars with perilous abandon as they whiz down the mountain from their morning training runs.

Something keeps drawing me, past the Valle di Susa and across the border into France. Past the Massif du Peloux, toward the unknown area on the map labeled Chaine de Belledonne and, beside it, the Massif de la Vanoise, winter playground for the rich, but now in summer oddly deserted to its vacant, postcard beauty.

I buy a topo map in a small store in St. Michel-de-Maurienne, park my car by a broad trailhead where a few French families are organizing picnic hampers. It's strange to move so swiftly from one language into another, like changing suddenly from salt water to fresh, a new element. The children nearby are diffident, silent, watching me already with the *haut bourgeois* mistrust of their elders toward a woman alone. I lace on my boots, fill a pack with toothbrush and sleeping bag, water and cereal bars, shrug off the curious looks of the

French, and set off, following nothing more than a small, tracked trail line on a map in a language I can barely read.

This landscape is gorgeous, almost too much so. It looks like the wrapper on a piece of Swiss chocolate: green meadows scattered with alpine blooms, snow-dusted peaks posing against a lupine-blue sky. The trail leads me up through the lingering afternoon light, higher and higher, past burbling streams that carve their calligraphy into the spare alpine geography. I am heading for the small triangle of a *refuge* near the peak of Val Thorens, Thor's mountain, the first place my glance landed as I perused the map, the coin's flip happening almost instinctively now.

Two hours later, dusty and sunburned, I round a bend and am poleaxed by the view. The *refuge*, a small stone hut, is perched like an eyrie on the edge of the world. Unfurling like a mist-blue apron around it, a panorama of snowy peaks and lavender valleys stretches into the distance. This is heaven. The sheer plunge of luck again.

The *refuge* manager, a young guy, checks me in, points to the bunk where I dump my gear. *Dinner at eight-thirty,* he tells me in a thick, Haute-Savoie accent. *We eat early for the climbers.* That's four hours away and, beautiful as it is there, I am still restless—so freed of my pack, I hike on to explore the trail beyond. The *refuge* guy says something about the spires, *a good walk, that way,* pointing to an indeterminate spot on the horizon.

The trail I take narrows above the first ridge, dips into and out of strangely quiet, windstill alpine valleys. All around, treeless peaks tower, catching the late sun on their craggy shoulders. The path goes up and up, the air sharpening, the vegetation growing dwarflike and stunted, a carpet of tiny flowers and tundra mosses, crouched and enduring. Patches of snow lie in the shade beneath boulders like scraps of leftover white cloth, and in the hollows the streams have a thin rime of ice along their banks. Gradually, I climb past all greenery, past timberline, into a world of rock and scree.

Over the lip of a rise, I come at last to the trail's end—a strange, opaque glacier lake, as still as the waters of Arthurian legend, set like an opal in a wide field of scattered rock, the broken bones of Thor's mountain. Piercing the sky directly ahead are the six bony spires of this peak, like six rigid fingers still counting off the six days of Creation, numbering the six weeks of my shattered, unexpected love. It occurs to me that I have come here to leave them, for safekeeping, in this beautiful, lifeless terrain. With sudden certainty, I know that we pass best through doorways empty handed; that whatever is to come, we can carry only the changes the past has forged in us, not its vessels or vestiges. Here in this high place, I feel my heart open and let him go, and like a long drawn breath released, free itself for the next inspiration.

. . .

LUCK AND LOVE. MY LOVER STIRS BESIDE ME, AND I FEEL US POISED FOR flight, the future before us veiled, the past clutched like papers of passage in our hands. God of thresholds. God of doorways. Doubt may not always be a sign that things are wrong. Sometimes it just signals that you must move forward, taking your uncertainty with you, mustering whatever grace and courage you can find.

Of course this story doesn't end in the Vanoise, not even its own small episode. Standing there those years ago, having set something important free, I wanted some sort of talisman of the moment, some souvenir of the place itself. *The first thing I see,* I told myself, shutting my eyes, then letting them open and land on . . . what *was* that? A dull glint in the rocks a few yards away, a shard of something I scrambled over to and bent to examine. It seemed a piece of brownish metal buried in shale. I dug down to get a purchase on it— my fingers closed around a cool, fat oblong—and I prodded and pulled its bulky form free of the gravel. When I stood up, I was holding a perfect, unexploded, foot-and-a-half-long mortar shell in my arms, heavy as a small child.

For a moment, I thought I might be about to blow us all—lake, scree, Thor's bony digits, and my six weeks of passion—into nothing more than granite ash and memory. I tried to remember anything I'd ever heard about explosives. I put my ear to it gently, as if trying to find a heartbeat. The quiet metal was cool against my cheek; it smelled like rust and rock. I decided, trusting to luck again, that it was safe, and then, as I looked around me across the scree field I began to make out more and more of them. Some were exploded, like eerie iron flowers blooming from deadly stamens; others were twisted from the incendiary heat, pockmarked, or shattered into oddly beautiful shards. The caps of some were missing, and their long cases had filled with sand. It was like a scattering of massive, broken bullets from the hand of some disgruntled deity.

You'll think me mad, but I hiked back down the mountain with my shell, my talisman, clumsy and comical in my arms. I had enough presence of mind to hide it in a cleft of rock a ways from the *refuge*, where I collected it the next morning and continued back down to my car, clutching it like a cumbersome, sleeping infant. It rolled around in my trunk for a few more weeks, my unwieldy bit of luck, my burdensome memento of letting things go. When I was ready to board my plane in Paris, I packed it into my carry-on with my copies of *Elle* and my bottle of Evian for the flight, plunked it down on the conveyer belt at the security checkpoint, and was startled at how quickly the gendarmes surrounded me when the alarm went off and the x-ray guy shouted, *Merde!*

We all looked at the frozen screen together. There were the ghostly skeletons of my cosmetics case and reading matter, the innocent grey ectoplasmic contents of my traveling bag—and there, in the center, the solid black form of the mortar shell, like a giant, lethal tumor in the fragile tissue of my Samsonite. I smiled at the gendarmes sheepishly. *Un souvenir. De la Vanoise.* They stared at me, uncomprehending. I tried another tack. *Je suis professeur de la histoire moderne. C'est un artifact de la guerre, vous comprenez?* They began to move me to the side, as graciously as only the French can handle the violent or the insane. *Mais Madame,* one murmured, *ça, ce n'est pas possible.*

There was a great deal of animated whispering and the agitations of bureaucracy as the officers sent messages up the line, asking first for someone superior to arrive and advise, then for someone trained in ballistics, then merely for someone who spoke English. Meanwhile, the x-ray guy had delicately removed the bomb from my bag and, holding it upside down like a large fountain pen, unscrewed the cap gingerly and with great concentration. We watched, a little breathless, as the device detached, and a small pile of alpine sand poured onto his shoes.

At last, someone clearly superior in rank arrived and addressed me with unctuous respect.

"Madame, there has been some misunderstanding. The artifacts of France are not to be removed from France. It is the law. We must ask that you surrender the *objet* to our authorities." I glanced at the x-ray man's loafers. "We will dispose of it with appropriateness."

Naturally, I agreed. I murmured my apologies and some words of cultural suasion, straightened my jacket a bit as if I'd been handled with more vigor than I really had. A gendarme rezipped and handed me my bag—abruptly and wonderfully lightened—but as I turned to go, the head official stopped me once more.

"*Un moment, s'il vous plait.* We must provide you documentation."

I looked at him.

"It is the law."

There was some shuffling and scribbling at a desk nearby. I thought of my six weeks ending twice, now three times—would they never be put to rest? I thought of the look on my lover's face as we parted: troubled, loving, uncertain. There was a signature, then another, followed by a couple of very official, resounding stamps. I wanted to spool back in time, back to the heat of an Italian summer, wine under a vine-covered pergola, a brocade of moonlight on a bed, the fury of new love, the wild ride of innocence and newfound luck. Back before the ache and creak of time set in.

The *fonctionnaire* tapped my shoulder, handed me a piece of paper that only after a few moments I was able to decipher.

"*Un reçu?*" I asked, disbelieving.

"*Oui, Madame.*"

"And may I then retrieve the object at some future time?"

"*Ah, non. Non, Madame.*" His brown eyes were kind, amused. "This is your receipt for something that can never be reclaimed."

⌣

The Weight of Spring Wind

Not long ago—five weeks, six—the last days of March brought what the French call *le débâcle*, ice breaking, the collapse of winter. Here in the Midwest, the ruin is rapid: one day nothing but blue light and air so thin it detonates with the gunshot sound of tree limbs cracking in the cold. The next day it's the debris-filled, coffee-colored waters of the Huron rushing to clear out a season's trash. On the lawn, the thaw reveals soggy thatch, dog shit and candy wrappers—was this what we were waiting for?

There is always the moment when everything changes. The moment things turn, and an intactness we don't even know to be grateful for is shattered—the moment of reversal, the one that by definition is its own decline.

I am sitting in an oncology clinic waiting room, waiting for the nurse to mispronounce my name as she always does, as she has done for the fourteen years I've been coming here since I had breast surgery in the spring of my thirtieth year. This is an unplanned, precipitous visit; there's been a change in my breast, and they've pushed aside other office visits in order to see me right away. I'm not sure I'm pleased at all at this preferential treatment, or at what it might imply.

Outside, the lilacs have begun to bloom; I can see them through the clinic's tinted windows, tossing their big heads in a wind I cannot feel or hear. I am encapsulated in a waiting area the color of a cultivated mushroom, the sofas dressed in soft mauve to mimic comfort.

When I found the lump this time, it was like something already known, awaited. The enemy you've been expecting for so long arrives, and it's a kind of relief. From this point on it will be war, something clear at least. It's such an odd ambivalence—the intimate invader, the body held close but turning against itself. The site of love and nurturance once more become a battlefield.

Sitting here, I tell myself stories: *You'll get through this. This isn't the worst.* I still have the scar from my breast surgery fourteen years ago. It is like a sliver of moon tracing the edge of my nipple, an ice-white shard of tissue without feeling now, a perfect curve, the kind that leaves no shadow.

I remember the last operation, blissed out on anesthesia until the local wore off, after which came pain so raw I had to gulp the air like a fish to get my breath.

The nurse emerges, stands for a moment peering at her clipboard.

It's spring again.

I want to screw my eyes shut and scream.

.   .   .

THERE IS ALWAYS THE MOMENT WHEN EVERYTHING REVERSES. I REMEMber once driving across western Colorado, a place called the Yampa Plateau, with the man I loved asleep in the passenger seat of my car. It was late afternoon, and there was a storm rumbling in the belly of the sky over the huge yellow horizon of the plains. I didn't know it then, but he was about to leave me for the second time. I guess I shouldn't have been surprised. But for now, I was ignorant and he was asleep—both states as close as either of us would get to innocence—and the sky above the Little Snake River was a vast swollen dusk of rain.

The road ran through the bluffs near the edge of the Elkhead Mountains, past the weird condos of a ski resort, like modern cliff-dwellings—identical stucco blocks the color of toast and a sea of balcony railings, regular as false teeth. The landscape faded back to ranchland, then to plains. The storm held off—just a few crazes of lightning high up inside the thunderheads. We passed through tiny towns made out of dirt and boredom. In one, a woman stood by the roadside and stared as we went past. She looked worn and poor—a sun-cracked, sullen face—but some nameless knowledge was in that gaze, as if she knew that even envy was just so much useless effort.

The land, bruised by the shadows of storm clouds, seemed endless. For optimists, space is about possibility; for pessimists, it is destitute, sheer lack. For someone like me at the time—neither optimist nor pessimist, but ironist—lack itself seemed a possibility, a reassuring sense of impermanence, a way to know how elemental and indistinguishable to the cosmos we are from a seed of gamma grass. There is a luxury in contemplating insignificance when one still feels loved, still feels that life is a horizon. A man is asleep beside a woman. The hour is rich with trust and calm. His soul is clean, her heart still poised toward his, unpierced by what is about to come.

I drove us up through Rabbit Ears Pass, across the lip of the Continental Divide, that defining line, a ridge on either side of which waters flow in opposite directions, heading back to different seas. There is always that pivot, the point of change. To the right of us, Muddy Creek roared its way toward Pueblo and rivers with names like Cucharas, Apishapa, Purgatoire; and then lightning finally split the sky like cracks in glaze, electricity tingled the air, my hair floating, my lover waking to the first huge splats of rain on the windshield.

. . .

THE DOCTOR IS GENTLE AS HE PERFORMS THE NEEDLE ASPIRATION, A BEE sting of pain just above my right nipple. I can't help noticing that my file is thick as a phone book.

He smiles. "Relax. We'll soon see what this is made of."

I don't want to know what I am made of. I resist this opening, this thaw. I fear what may emerge—what refuse, what dead things, what strange new growth.

. . .

I TELL MYSELF STORIES. I HAVE A HOUSE, A JOB, BOOKS TO WRITE, A LIFE. The season has fast-forwarded again. I sit on my back porch and watch my patch of world change.

That last spring, too, the transformation had been fast. We had been monitoring a lump I'd found nearly eighteen months before, which for a while seemed to be stable. Then, in five weeks, its size doubled. "We're going in," my surgeon said, as if announcing a military maneuver.

It was all very quick. The forms to sign, the instructions. Then I was lying on a gurney staring at the pre-op lights that looked like landing UFOs, like dishes filled with some new, luminous chemical, while a masked, brisk nurse scrubbed me with orange disinfectant.

Not *me*—my breast. My clavicle, sternum, rib cage. For the first time in my life, I was a body, a thing, being prepared for the knife. I was a system that could fail, a mechanism that could be separated from my sentient self as easily as placing a surgical tent between my gaze and the incision.

Numbed with lidocaine, when the cut came I could feel the scalpel only as a dull tug. Robbed of its sting, it was something happening to someone else, a hundred miles away. A nurse was humming the tune from a shaving cream commercial, the only other sounds the click of surgical instruments on a metal tray, the buzz of fluorescence from the lights above. My surgeon's eyes were kind above her mask:

"Later, we'll give you codeine for the pain." What pain? I was a rubber doll, a lump of clay, a gag body like a fake Halloween hand on a car seat. I would never feel myself again.

. . .

What is the weight of spring wind? SHANJU, MY ZEN TEACHER, ASKED US once. A koan, a riddle, unanswerable. Spring wind heavy with aroma, freighted with memories. How much does expectation weigh?

. . .

ALL THAT DAY AND THE NEXT I WAIT FOR THE LAB RESULTS FROM THE clinic. The sky is a haze, the air muggy. Seeds drift like lint.

There's no word by afternoon, so I go to my ceramics class to stay occupied. The unseasonable moisture gets into everything: the walls of my bowl collapse, stray hairs are glued to my forehead, my eyelids. From the side, the woman at the wheel next to me looks like a little girl, head bowed, eyes intent on the vase that eludes her fingers. She smooths her brow with the back of her hand, looks up and smiles to show a glimpse of aging beauty. Even as we kill time, it goes on fashioning us.

Tosca competes with Miles Davis on a funky radio, while our teacher gazes out the studio door at the daylight that glazes and spackles this unfinished world. Slowly, I start over, pull a cylinder upward from its unformed mass. The whirling puck of clay—straight and motionless in the flywheel's hum—waits to take its shape and rise.

I try to focus on concentric things, things spinning outward from a base—thoughts, gestures, memory, family, love, this spinning planet tipped precariously into its seasons, but somehow still centered. I remember the perfect basin of a pond at dawn, swimming with the mist rising in tendrils like steam off tea-colored water, the loons paddling before me, silent after a night of strange music, V's of water trailing them like silver ribbon. A pond round as an eye, and a morning equally concentric: blue iridescence around a dark center.

Like a living being, the clay anticipates the next thing, the image of imposed form. Concentrate. I remember climbing the Old Man of Storr in Scotland, high above where a wild sea slavered against the rocks. Around me, cold skirls of autumn wind fluting the blowholes of volcanic rock; below me, one golden eagle wheeling, tracing circle after circle on the blue body of morning air.

Shape is also what isn't there, my teacher says. A bowl is formed by absence. She holds a straight edge across the lip of clay—*watch how the light bends: the test of a true sphere is its shadow.* Just so our days: bowls filled with light, cut by the sliver of darkness that defines.

I think about the whorls and spheres of a painting that hangs above my bed, one passionate gash of red bisecting an abstract field of blues. The woman who painted it was a nun. Her sister, too, had been in a convent, somewhere outside of Pittsburgh, where in 1994 she was found raped and strangled in the woods behind the mother house. Her sister, the artist, left the order and painted a series of watercolors titled "The Last Things Joanna Saw": trees; sun; the blue, unwinking eye of heaven.

And I knew a woman whose daughter fell from the Cliffs of Moher. The girl was only eighteen, with a group of other exchange students on a field trip to the west coast of Ireland. They'd been on a bus all morning, and in the excitement, the cluster and push of youngsters eager to stretch their legs and see the view, the group bustling up behind her made her lose her footing, pitch unbelievably past the lip of rock 600 feet over the ocean to her death.

I heard this story twenty years ago, sitting at a formica table in the basement lunchroom of the bank where the dead girl's mother and I both worked. Three or four of us sat with sandwiches and salads untouched while this ordinary woman—a teller, like us—revisited that history, quietly imagined the last moment her daughter's foot had contact with earth, and that other last moment, the instant her own life—as a mother, as a woman—stepped off the precipice of grief past which it would fall forever.

The shape under my fingers careens and collapses, floppy as grey leather. Death takes you off-center; once you begin to wobble, you cannot right yourself. We tell ourselves stories, spin our way out of this impossible darkness. Our bodies, these delicate envelopes into which life is slipped like a love letter. Outside the studio, a grackle lands in a tree, chuck-chuck-chucking, then commits its odd song, a sound like a rusty hinge opening.

I begin again, throw the slick clay. It feels like flesh, like muscle.

Inside me is a little fist of fear. When the scalpel draws its fine line, I think red heat will erupt from my body just like that, like going through earth's mantle to its core.

. . .

AFTER THE ANESTHESIA WORE OFF—THAT FIRST TIME, THAT LAST TIME, fourteen years ago—I stepped off a cliff of pain. It was like falling through a purple sea, gyrating, my body twisting. The codeine only slurred my mind; the pain was smarter now, not to be tricked. It took up lodging somewhere deeper than my nerves and far beyond the sliced flesh that throbbed beneath bandages. The pain moved in with me somewhere untouchable.

But deeper than that, I felt as if someone had peeled off a layer of my soul. There had been a moment, a segment of time, now gone, in which I had still been whole, undamaged, integral. What was it I wanted back again? Surely not the renegade mass, that filigree of crazy cells that could still write out my life sentence.

The lump had been bigger than the surgeon expected. "This one was a real lollapaloosa," she said. They dropped it in a jar. "Do you want to see it?"

Why did the idea of looking at a rejected part of myself, grey and refracted in formaldehyde, terrify me? I imagined the lump as a tiny brain on one of those late-night movie channels, suspended in fluid, still pulsing its evil, bodiless instructions. Surely that had been worth taking away. But with the invader had also gone the immunity; it was as if being intact itself had once—irrationally, incredibly— been the magic amulet preserving me.

. . .

WINTER WAS SAFETY, A STRING OF FROZEN MOMENTS. AS IF TIME COULD drop anchor, could be caught in a fist of ice. Now cottonwoods explode with seed, days regain velocity. Memory rushes past like meltwater, filled with its own debris.

· · ·

When I was a child, I wore a gold medallion my mother had brought back from Lourdes, a medal of the Virgin, whom Bernadette called *Aquero,* "That One." *O Mary conceived without sin pray for us who have recourse to thee.* My mother visited Lourdes often as a girl. I think she liked the idea of sacred celebrity.

When my parents went out of town, sometimes they would leave my sister and me with the nuns. The cavernous convent was a magical place—gleaming linoleum the color of chocolate, the lurid statues of wounded saints in niches on the stairwells. Each morning at five o'clock the bell would ring for the nuns to come to matins, and the same novitiate, Sister Cyrena, would peek into our room to tell us to go back to sleep. We'd lie there gazing at the boughs of the convent's huge pines, blue-black in the dawn light, warm still under the frugal sheets, feeling marvelously *in* this place but not *of* it.

It was Sister Cyrena who, one evening at bathtime, insisted on removing my medallion as I was getting in the tub. I resisted—I had never had it off—and when I flinched from her, the thing we both feared happened. Together we watched the gold chain snake down the drain, glittering for an instant against the porcelain, then shimmering, shortening, gone, the Virgin disappearing like a yellow lozenge down the dull brass throat of the convent's plumbing.

Never mind, the sister said uncertainly. It was the quaver of guilt in her voice that made me start to cry. A wary child, I recognized that tremor—the nun suddenly no more than a girl caught, expecting to be punished. Her eyes were big and blue; I think I must have frightened her with my sorrow. But in my child's mind, I believed she was staring at me and my sudden vulnerability: one minute safe, the next stripped entirely of miraculous protection.

Later, when I was in bed, she came to soothe me. She tried to show me her hair under her cowl—it was meant to be a treat, no doubt, a strange gift, perhaps all she had to offer. I stared at the unkempt tangle, cropped like a boy's, brown salted prematurely with grey—and the raw, unprotected privacy of that gesture made me cry all over again.

. . .

VIALS OF CHRIST'S TEARS, THE BREATH OF JUDAS, DUST FROM THE fingernails of Roland or Charlemagne. I think sometimes that faith is a quarrel with the void, conducted in a language unknown to the void. Things in their unwinnable argument with oblivion.

My mother still has two murky bottles of Lourdes water she keeps under a print of Michelangelo's *Pietà*. In the picture, Christ's limbs are elegant as an athlete's, but Mary looks startled, holding this sprawling man's body in her lap—baffled, as if he'd fallen there from the sky. How young she looks, younger even than her son, a mere girl to whom these inconceivable things—motherhood, divinity, this agony of loss—have simply happened.

I know all about what might befall me; I've done my reading. Say the word: *cancer.* No avoidance for me; I don't want to be surprised. Though maybe research is just a more refined denial, a different form of prayer, pressing bald truth like flowers between the covers of medical journals.

The words are a rune. I recite them and they become the names of exotic plants: *hyperplasia, fibroadenoma, epithelial carcinomatosis.* When the hospital calls, I will be ready—I know terms, I understand the options, laid out like an algorithm.

But when it finally comes, the news is tricky. The lab results, they tell me on the phone, are inconclusive. Not enough cells? The wrong cells? My doctor wants to operate, an excisional biopsy. "Why leave it in there like a time bomb, since we don't know what it is? In and out. Then we'll be sure."

Time bomb. The body's uncertainty. Black mass going on in this temple. In the shower, my hand travels over my breast—my fingers make a flat raft, pressing, circling inward. There. Hard, like a coin under my skin, a gate of horn. My self, split from itself, fissuring.

. . .

They want one more mammogram before the procedure, and I descend into the catacombs of the Radiology Department to comply. I get on the elevator with a young mother and her son, the little boy in a wheelchair, his chest arched like a small chicken's. He's wearing a Detroit Red Wings cap, and tubes come out of his arms like electrical wiring.

In Mammography, women are shuffled from space to space—called from the outer waiting room to change into gowns, then to resettle and wait some more in an inner waiting room where the magazines are all about holiday crafts and recipes, and the TV is permanently tuned to *Days of Our Lives*. We look like a strange order of devotionals, dressed in our lumpy, pale blue habits, tactfully avoiding each other's gaze. There are brochures about menopause and venereal disease that nobody touches.

The soap opera's plot creeps forward. One by one we are moved again, this time to inner sancta, each woman to her own mammography room to contemplate in solitude the giant glass-plated machine, big as an industrial die stamper, its cone of radiation lowered, discretely waiting.

Strange how the body as object can become either derelict or sacred. Sometimes less, sometimes more than itself. Odd that the words *venery* and *veneration* stem from one root. And how we use fragments to symbolize integrity: Saint Lucia holding her eyes on a plate, the severed breasts of Saint Anne. *Ex voto* offerings of arms, legs, plastic replicas of kidneys, tiny crutches hanging from church walls. Amulets. Human synecdoche. Parts for the whole.

Poor Bernadette was a girl much photographed as well. They exhumed her body three times to demonstrate to unbelieving potentates the state of her miraculous preservation. She's on permanent display now, in a glass casket in St. Gildard's in Burgundy, where busloads of curious tourists are unloaded three times a day. Her corpse was washed and dressed by the nuns, her eyebrows plucked, her face made up. Her kneecaps, liver, diaphragm, and two ribs have been removed mysteriously over the years, vandalized for relics.

The nurse comes in: *Hello*— she looks down, reads out my name from her file. *This won't take a minute. I expect you know the drill.* We slip the gown from my right side; I grasp the machine's plastic handle, feel the nurse flatten my breast against the plate as if it were a knot of dough. Smooth, professional. The glass plates come together, pinning me painfully. How many women before me have stood here cursing this machine? The nurse retreats into her safety booth. Not her; she's immune.

The radiation zips through me, and the machine lets me go. I am no longer the object of its short attention, its brief embrace. I am shuffled off through a different door to wait until the nurse is sure the pictures took, then down an unfamiliar corridor, back to the changing room again, out to Cashier's and Referrals, up the elevators, through the lobby and the brilliant turnstile doors, back inexplicably into the blinking sun.

. . .

NEXT DAY THE SKY IS THIN-SHELLED AND BLUE AS A WREN'S EGG, AND the pear blossoms that fell in last night's rain have made the lawn look like church steps after a wedding. My pear tree is old; most of its branches are dead. Just a scurf of green along its outer twigs, where life will push itself out one more year in a snowfall of flowers, a few diminished bronze globes of fruit. By frost they'll be bursting with juice and taste like everything that combined to make them—autumn sun, July's cut grass, the cold faint nectar of last year's spring wind.

My parents have come in from out of town to be with me for the surgical procedure. They are ensconced in a Marriott Hotel nearby, insisting on leaving me my privacy, calling every hour or two to tell me so. This morning my mother has gone shopping; my father visits with me and we have coffee on my deck. I find myself thinking, ungenerously, that he should be the patient, not me. The backs of his hands are spotted, and his hair has begun to look ghostly—white and insubstantial as mist. It's lonely hearing him talk to himself, watching him comfort himself by arguing medical probabilities with me. He lowers his eyes and turns away, as he has done so many times before. The words *biopsy, mastectomy* scare him, a fact he blatantly tries to hide.

What is the heft of something ever moving, carrying time on its back? All my life I have invented stories to explain my father's reticence. I am tough, to guard myself from too much disappointment. Even now, words shield me. I sit on the deck and think *lilac trees, bony as farm women* and *robin's breast the color of dried blood, the color of Christ's promises*. Age, like spring, sharpens all the battle lines. In the merciless May sun, I realize my father is disappearing a little more each day.

. . .

I THINK OF ANOTHER SPRING, AN EARLY JUNE, HIKING THE INYO WILDERNESS in California's High Sierras. In a riverbed above King's Canyon, we found the looped cursive of animal tracks—chamois and lynx—first paced, then circling, then intertwined as in a dance. The carcass was gone, not even the slow spiral of a buzzard to break up the flat blue sky.

The friend I was with, a physician I had known since his medical school days, told me stories he'd come across in his research: tropical diseases, viral infections, bacteria that turn you into jelly from the inside out. *The wonder,* he said, *is really that we live as long as we do.* Our bodies, such permeable vessels we steer without thinking into the path of strange forces.

This same man, my friend, was a mountain climber who had once been caught in an avalanche while making an ascent of Denali's east face. The team had rigged a guyline across a snowfield, and my friend was halfway to the ridge when he heard above him the deafening locomotive rumble of his death charging at him in the form of a tsunami of snow. All he could do was wrap his arm around the guyline in the seconds before the avalanche hit, and cup his free hand over his nose and mouth to buy another minute or two of oxygen before he died.

When the snow covered him, although his eyes were shut, he said the world turned blue. The pressure of half a mountain was compacted over and around him; he felt his ribs bend and crack, and in the preternatural silence after the din of settling snow, he heard one loud pop, which was the sound of his arm, still wrapped in guyline, leaving its socket. In that one moment, of all things, he suddenly realized that he was in love with a woman who until then he had known only socially—he could envision her clearly, in a friend's kitchen in Sausalito, tearing the leaves for a salad, looking over her shoulder and laughing at something someone had said. He could see with such precision her hair, the light on her skin, the very fabric of the skirt she was wearing. *What a shit*, he thought, *to die now.*

He felt cold fingers curling around his heart, felt himself blacking out. Just then, the snow, inexplicably, heaved past itself, slid into a second avalanche that pulled on down the mountain and left him free, hanging from the guywire, blinking in the miraculous, sudden sun.

The moment of reversal. Remission. Pardon. The moment after which nothing is ever again the same.

That night in the Inyo, the stars were chips of ice in a frozen sky, the Milky Way a spume of light, food from the distant breast of space. We had camped near the trail, a wavering grey ribbon that gradually vanished into the darkness. I asked my friend what had become of the woman. He said, after he'd gotten out of the hospital in Anchorage, he flew back to San Francisco and went to her.

He told her straight, in words as clear as he could find, about his experience, about his love for her. Everything he'd felt—about death, about his own life—was distilled into that declaration. He stood there like Lazarus and felt the universe coming to a point, a pivot. He thought that at any moment his heart too might give a loud crack and explode from its socket with the pressure, the importance of this change.

But the truth is, other people's crises are banal. It's like someone who's just been in a plane crash trying to explain the experience to somebody sitting by a pool. It simply doesn't work. The woman just looked at him blankly, as if she were having trouble placing him. Then she said she already had a boyfriend, and she wasn't interested in a doctor's late hours. She didn't even ask him in.

So he turned around and went back home. But it was odd, he said—as he walked back to his car, it was as if he had stepped out of his own body and was watching himself from a distance: a rejected man with his arm in a sling walking back to his car. He felt no regret and very little involvement. It was the snow's strange gift: the self divided from itself, familiar, foreign, observant.

Years later, he met the woman he would marry, and he said it was worth the wait to find the person who could love you back as deeply as you loved them. They'd been together now for seventeen years, had three beautiful children. But sometimes even now, he said, he'd be lying in bed beside her, or be placing his hand on hers just as the lights dimmed in a concert hall, and he would again take that step outside his own life and find himself looking back, watching himself like a third person, loving and being loved.

Perhaps when you step across that threshold once, forever after the doorway stays a little bit ajar. We gazed at the dark silhouettes of chaparral, the luminous crescent of Palisade Glacier. I thought how easy it is to become lost in this landscape, this syntax of wild forms, this journey whose ending is written in a code we cannot understand.

. . .

SPRING IS THE SEASON FOR PILGRIMAGE. CHAUCER'S SOFT APRIL, HIS *showres soote.* Compostela: field of stars.

They say it is about connection: rejoining body and spirit, metaphor and actuality, coupling the inner journey with a real one across time and landscape. Hiking to higher ground.

My mother went back often to Lourdes. Later in life, when she developed masses in her breasts like me, she flew Lufthansa back to Europe—not to a shrine, but to a spa town with a good surgeon for a lumpectomy, because American doctors in the sixties still thought of radical mastectomy as the treatment of choice. Unsentimental pilgrimage: my mother's own palmer's journey to stay intact.

She was still young then, pretty. Age and disfigurement terrified her. I remember her, still in her thirties, sitting at her dressing table plucking the premature grey hairs from her head until my father joked he'd rather have her grey than bald. As a girl, she'd been afraid of the *malades*—their rigid, aimless faces, the way they were parked and perambulated all through Lourdes, a traffic jam of stretchers and wheelchairs. But the Virgin, she said, was beautiful—a wonder, that blue sash, those red roses on her tiny feet.

Our Lady doesn't interest me, her crown of stars, her gold-tipped basilica. Instead, I know that for an entrance fee you can walk through the hovel where Bernadette had lived—sixth child of grinding poverty, four to a bed, choleric, tubercular, mud floors, no light, a girl for whom fresh water was enough of a miracle. Why is it *she* who calls to me, who beckons us all to cross over our sea of self-pity?

They say it is about connection: our momentary troubles dignified as they echo a more timeless *via dolorosa.* How many thousands have walked these stones, have lain upon these surfaces, asking to be healed? It is to salve the rift between the one and the rest, between moment and history—to cross thresholds worn to a gleam by other travelers' feet, marble softened by millennia of human hands and hopes brushing the knees, the lips, the miters of saints' statues.

Something imperishable calls to us. Yesterday in a shopping mall,

I passed three Buddhist monks standing in front of Radio Shack in robes the color of nasturtium. Without thinking, I bowed to them as I walked past. How they beamed and rebeamed, touching fingertips to lips, to foreheads, to acknowledge the divinity of the human across time, across gender and race, across the space between us.

. . .

I'M TOLD TO FAST THE NIGHT BEFORE SURGERY, LIKE A PILGRIM, EATING, drinking nothing, no alcohol, no aspirin, no drugs. I have to empty myself out, becoming nothing again but muscle, sinew, bone.

I am instructed to remove all jewelry—if my heart fails and they need to apply the paddles, electricity can arc through silver or gold and burn the flesh beneath it. It surprises me how every ring is weighted with association. With each one I take off, I strip myself of a memory that had been bound to me by its precious metal—tokens of love and anniversary. Isn't this divestiture itself a kind of failure of the heart?

Nothing unnecessary, the nurse had said.

. . .

7:00 A.M. MY MOTHER CAN'T DECIDE WHICH SHOES TO WEAR TO THE hospital. My father fusses about the books he'll take to pass the time. They are like children going on an outing, my elderly parents. Through the stream of the shower, I can hear them quarreling about who should drive.

We arrive by 7:45. There are already a surprising number of people there; the lobby seems crowded as a bus station. The receptionist points us to the waiting area, explains directions to the pharmacy—*for later.* She invites my parents to help themselves to coffee and fresh muffins. *And you're the patient?* She tilts her hairdo at me. I nod. *You can have water. The fountain's over there by Chemo.*

We find places, settle into the plush, squeakless upholstery. Phones are bleating everywhere. I try to read an article in an old

Smithsonian, but my fingers seem to keep turning the magazine's edges to damp pulp. My father blows on his coffee. My mother looks at her shoes, tilting them this way and that as if she's contemplating a purchase. None of us speaks.

After twenty minutes there is sudden activity. A heavyset nurse bustles over with a file, and the three of us stand up in unison.

"Are you the Marcolinos?"

"No."

"Sorry. So sorry."

Awkwardly, we sit back down. We must look interchangeable. *A good thing they asked,* my father says ominously.

One by one the patients are called away. Their loved ones look immensely left behind—they fiddle or stand, suddenly unmoored, and walk around the lobby or out the silent, automatic doors to pace the curb, trying to stay out of the path of wheelchairs. They look so lost, the healthy, in this temple of disease.

At ten to nine, the right nurse finally comes for me. My mother takes my jacket; I kiss her papery, dry cheek. She feels so ethereal. My father pats my shoulder with a frail hand. When did they let themselves get so old? I turn and read my nurse's nametag—*Rosaria*—then follow her through the large metal doors into whatever's next.

From the waiting room to pre-op is sheer inversion, like stepping through a membrane into an alternate world. The colors change, from pastel plums and pinks to ice white and sterile blue, and the muted gab of Muzak switches to the clink of instruments, the clean hum of rubber wheels on linoleum. After the stale tension of the waiting room, the smells here are brisk and tannic, like there's been a rain. The nurses are friendly without the usual false edge of hospital cheer.

Rosaria hands me a bundle—hospital socks and gown—and it's almost a relief to take off street clothes and assume the shift of the generic, the penitent, booted and blanketed like a baby, raised into bed, adjusted, tucked, hands laid upon you with skilled beneficence. Soon I'm lying back, warm, listening to patients banter gently with each other in this last, safe space. *When do the bacon and eggs get served? I don't know about you, honey, but I plan to go out dancing tonight.* Their voices float to me from behind the separating curtains, like the gentle, disembodied sounds of souls departed. If heaven has a foyer, it will be soft and transitional as this place, unhurried, sweet and warm as fresh laundry.

Rosaria leans over my bed, asks how I'm doing. Her accent is rich and crisp, her smile beautiful. They will begin to prep me now, she says.

Another nurse cups my wrist, taps the back of my hand to raise a vein. I know this time they will be using Demerol. Calm hands attach electrodes, and we begin to see my heart spike and rest in a green line on the monitor.

I try to hold onto this moment, the last one before we fizz into the future. It's this instant before the cut I want to catch—that moment of integrity, eternal, evanescent, forever suspended and forever destroyed by its own definition, erased in its own movement to completion. But I have nothing to hold it with; I am reduced to nerve and tendon, blood pressure, a pulse on a machine. The pilgrims took nothing with them into the journey. A staff, a scallop shell, the hope that they would find provision.

Hands move over and around me, reassuring. I look up at the wide white of a nurse's uniform, at the end of which are Rosaria's eyes.

When will you give me the anesthesia?

She looks down at me, smiles.

We already have.

Then we are in motion, all of us together, a strange processional, the IV rattling like a skinny mendicant, my gurney a white raft, a litter borne forward by gentle, gloved hands. The needle drips its dreams. *I think she's under.* But I'm not; it's just that the doctors have orange robes and roses on their feet.

It's then that I feel it, cool and fresh, with the sting of snow still in it: blowing the storm clouds over Cucharas, blowing rain into a dusty Colorado town, herding the Arctic light around the sky, rushing down the valley of the river Gave, mysterious freshness, gentling the fixed, lost look of the paralytic. Zephyr combing my mother's beautiful grey hair, stroking her aging body into peace, lifting my father's white wisps and fluttering the pages of the book in his hands until he can no longer look down and away. In my twilight sleep I feel its soft gust move around and over us as we wheel down the hospital corridor, making the nurses think for a moment of wings and heartbeats not mapped out on a screen, the sleep of someone loved beneath their arms. Under the force of its gentle inspiration, ice shatters, white fields break into blossom. There is always the moment, because every moment is the one beyond which nothing is the same. The weight of spring wind blows open the swinging door, and inside a girl who was me, hair floating, red skirt billowing, is laughing at the world in motion, laughing at a universe of falling petals.

Notes

1. Ted Hughes, *Selected Poems, 1957–1994* (New York: Farrar, Straus & Giroux, 2002), 41.

2. Ibid.

3. Ntosake Shange, *For colored girls who have considered suicide/when the rainbow is enuf* (New York: Macmillan, 1977), 50.

4. Thomas Merton, *Learning to Love: The Journals of Thomas Merton, vol. 6, 1966–1967* (San Francisco: Harper Collins, 1997).

5. *The Essential Haiku: Versions of Basho, Buson and Issa,* ed. Robert Hass (Hopewell, N.J.: The Ecco Press, 1994), 56.

6. Ibid, 70.

7. Ibid, 57–58.

8. Ibid, 58.

9. Robert Boyle, *The Hudson River: A Natural and Unnatural History* (New York: Norton, 1969), 34. Many of the facts and anecdotes paraphrased in this chapter originated from this text.

10. Ibid, 16.

11. Ambrose Bierce, *The Devil's Dictionary* (New York: Albert & Charles Boni, 1911), 42.

12. Boyle, *The Hudson River,* 32–33.

13. Ibid, 30.

14. Ibid, 45.

15. Ibid, 42.

16. Ibid, 62.
17. Thomas Merton, *Learning to Love*, 306.
18. Ibid, 313.
19. Ibid, 327.
20. Ibid, 305–6, 336.
21. Wallace Stevens, *The Collected Poems of Wallace Stevens* (New York: Knopf, 1954), 521.
22. Merton, *Learning to Love*, 307.
23. Stevens, *The Collected Poems*, 520.

Acknowledgments

An excerpt from "Falling Bodies" first appeared in *The Notre Dame Review* (2002) under the title "Humus"

"Anything" and "The Secret Lives of Fish" first appeared in *Gulf Coast* (2001)

"Investments" first appeared in *Cream City Review* (1999)

"Grace" first appeared in *The Literary Review* (1997)

"Theft and Loss" first appeared in *New Letters Magazine* (2002)

"Preservation: A Story" first appeared in *The Notre Dame Review* (2004)

An excerpt from "Preservation: A Story" first appeared in *Juggler* (1982) under the title "Unfinished"

An excerpt from "Men at Fifty" first appeared in *Juggler* (1981) under the title "Tribunal"

"The Weight of Spring Wind" first appeared in *New Millennium Writings* (2001)

green
press
INITIATIVE

Michigan State University Press is committed to preserving ancient forests and natural resources. We have elected to print this title on New Leaf EcoOffset 100, which is 100% recycled (100% post-consumer waste) and processed chlorine free (PCF). As a result of our paper choice, Michigan State University Press has saved the following natural resources*:

47	Trees (40 feet in height)
2,233	Pounds of Solid Waste
20,024	Gallons of Water
34	Million BTUs of Energy
4,401	Pounds of Greenhouse Gases
12	Pounds of Air Emissions (HAPs, VOCs, TRSs combined)
138	Pounds of Hazardous Effluent (BODs, TSSs, CODs, and AOXs combined)

We are a member of Green Press Initiative—a nonprofit program dedicated to supporting book publishers in maximizing their use of fiber that is not sourced from ancient or endangered forests. For more information about Green Press Initiative and the use of recycled paper in book publishing, please visit *www.greenpressinitiative.org*.

*Environmental benefits are calculated by New Leaf Paper based on research done by the Environmental Defense Fund and other members of the Paper Task Force who study the environmental impacts of the paper industry.

DATE DUE

PROVIDENCE ATHENAEUM

AUG 1 7 2004